# WORKING IT OUT

## INTERACTIVE ENGLISH FOR THE WORKPLACE

RONNA MAGY

**Heinle & Heinle Publishers**

I T P  **An International Thomson Publishing Company**

**Pacific Grove • Albany • Bonn • Boston • Cincinnati • Detroit • London • Madrid • Melbourne
Mexico City • New York • Paris • San Francisco • Tokyo • Toronto • Washington**

*This book is dedicated to those who study and work*

*— Ronna Magy*

The publication of *Working It Out: Interactive English for the Workplace* was directed by the members of Heinle & Heinle Secondary and Adult ESL Publishing Team:

Editorial Director: Jeri Cipriano
Production Services Coordinator: Mike Burggren
Market Development Directors: Jonathan Boggs and
  Thomas Dare
Also participating in the program were:
Vice President and Publisher, ESL: Stanley Galek
Managing Developmental Editor: Amy Lawler

Associate Developmental Editor: Sally Conover
Director of Global ELT Training: Evelyn Nelson
Manufacturing Coordinator: Mary Beth Hennebury
Interior Designer/Compositor: PC&F, Inc.
Cover Designer: Mike Burggren and Jeff Cosloy Design
Illustrator: Rod Thomas
Photographers: Silvio Parodi and Jonathan Stark

Manufactured in the United States of America.

ISBN: 08384-8135-3

Heinle & Heinle is a division of International Thomson Publishing, Inc.

# Contents

# CONTENTS

| Higher Order Thinking Skills and Strategies | Work Culture Notes | Language Structures (in text and Grammar Appendix) |
|---|---|---|
| ■ predict a story from the title and pictures<br>■ compose a letter looking for a job<br>■ identify and evaluate personality traits<br>■ make a graph of job selection factors<br>■ evaluate job applicants | ■ Personality<br>*Put your best foot forward* | For more help using **descriptive adjectives,** turn to p. 113 in the Grammar Appendix |
| ■ predict events in a story<br>■ compose questions about a story<br>■ interpret a diagram<br>■ read a graph<br>■ compose paragraphs | ■ Making Contact, Making Friends<br>*Have a positive attitude* | For more help **making Wh- and How questions,** turn to p. 114 in the Grammar Appendix |
| ■ predict a story from questions<br>■ collect and interpret information<br>■ identify the topic of a paragraph<br>■ compose opinion paragraphs<br>■ read a graph<br>■ problem solve | ■ The Changing Technology of the Workplace<br>*Skills and retraining*<br>■ Job Changes and New Careers | For more help **talking about experience using the present perfect,** turn to p. 115 in the Grammar Appendix |
| ■ scan a story for information<br>■ make a bar graph<br>■ evaluate reportable information<br>■ make inferences from information<br>■ formulate sentences about work problems | ■ Communication between a Worker and a Boss<br>*Efficiency and flexibility* | For more help **asking for clarification,** turn to p. 116 in the Grammar Appendix |
| ■ scan a story for information<br>■ compose a paragraph<br>■ create timelines<br>■ analyze a chart<br>■ evaluate reasons for leaving a job | ■ Changing Jobs—Starting a New Career<br>*Take a personal inventory* | For more help **talking about the past,** turn to p. 117 in the Grammar Appendix |
| ■ preview a story by asking questions<br>■ evaluate reasons to take a day off<br>■ problem solve<br>■ summarize information<br>■ edit a story | ■ Pay Stub<br>■ The Fair Labor Standards Act | For more help **summarizing information,** turn to p. 118 in the Grammar Appendix |
| ■ preview a story by looking for information<br>■ retell a story<br>■ compose a memo to a safety committee<br>■ read and interpret a graph<br>■ fill out an industrial accident report | ■ Health and Safety: The Occupational Safety and Health Act of 1970 | For more help **requesting help,** turn to p. 119 in the Grammar Appendix |
| ■ predict a story from answers to questions<br>■ take notes from a speech<br>■ edit a story<br>■ compile a survey<br>■ interpret a statement of medical benefits | ■ Labor Unions<br>*rights and representation*<br>■ Federal laws protecting working people<br>■ Medical Benefits | For more help **asking about a period of time,** turn to p. 120 in the Grammar Appendix |

# SCANS AND

## United States Department of Labor Secretary's

| Skills | Basic Skills | Thinking Skills | Personal Qualities | Resource Management | |
|---|---|---|---|---|---|
| CHAPTER 1<br>Looking for and Finding a Job | X | X | X | X | |
| CHAPTER 2<br>Starting a New Job | X | X | X | — | |
| CHAPTER 3<br>Technology and Training | X | X | X | — | |
| CHAPTER 4<br>Communicating with Your Boss | X | X | X | X | |
| CHAPTER 5<br>Work in My Home Country, Work in My New Country | X | X | X | X | |
| CHAPTER 6<br>Work Schedules and Paychecks | X | X | X | X | |
| CHAPTER 7<br>Safety | X | X | X | — | |
| CHAPTER 8<br>Labor Unions, Labor Laws, and Benefits | X | X | X | — | |

**CASAS COMPETENCIES**

**4.1** Understand basic principles of getting a job
**4.2** Understand wages, benefits, and concepts of employee organizations
**4.3** Understand work-related safety standards and procedures
**4.4** Understand concepts and materials related to job performance and training
**4.5** Effectively utilize common workplace technology and systems

(CASAS = Comprehensive Adult Student Assessment System)

# CASAS CORRELATIONS

## Commission of Achieving Necessary Success

| Interpersonal Skills | Information Management | Systems Management | Technology | CASAS Competencies |
|:---:|:---:|:---:|:---:|:---:|
| X | X | — | — | 4.1 |
| X | — | — | X | 4.4 |
| X | X | — | X | 4.3<br>4.4<br>4.5 |
| X | X | X | — | 4.6<br>4.8<br>4.9 |
| X | — | — | — | 4.1<br>4.4<br>4.8<br>4.9 |
| X | X | X | — | 4.2<br>4.6 |
| X | X | X | X | 4.3  4.7<br>4.4  4.9<br>4.5 |
| X | X | X | — | 4.2<br>4.8<br>4.9 |

**4.6** Communicate effectively in the workplace
**4.7** Effectively manage workplace resources
**4.8** Demonstrate effectiveness in working with other people
**4.9** Understand how social, organizational, and technological
systems work, and operate effectively within them

*Working It Out* covers all of
the vocational topics in
connection with the
California Model Standards

# TO THE TEACHER

*Working It Out: Interactive English for the Workplace* is a workplace-literacy text with audiotape for intermediate level students. These materials empower students to function in the changing workplace with its focus on technology, teamwork, and individual responsibility.

*Working It Out* is designed for:

- Vocational classrooms
- English as a Second Language classrooms with vocational component
- Vocational ESL (VESL) classrooms
- Workplace ESL programs.

*Working It Out* focuses students on the nature and culture of the American workplace.

▶ Chapters 1 and 2, "Looking for and Finding a Job" and "Starting a New Job," orient the student to the job search process and the cultural nuances of the work environment.

▶ Chapters 3 and 4, "Technology and Training" and "Communicating with Your Boss," guide students through the many interpersonal and technological skills needed in the workplace.

▶ Chapter 5, "Work in My Home Country, Work in My New Country," assists students in comparing work in their native countries with work in the United States and in setting goals for their futures.

▶ Chapters 6, 7, and 8, "Work Schedules and Paychecks," "Safety," and "Labor Unions, Labor Laws, and Benefits," expose students to the essential components of the workplace.

**Challenge activities,** the activities for higher level learners within each chapter, are labeled with an asterisk (★).

The **Grammar Appendix** gives students the opportunity to expand their grammar practice with level-appropriate language structures that appear in the text. **Focused Listening Activities** appear in each chapter. Students listen to situations and conversations among workers and bosses. Problem solving and role play activities are developed from those conversations. In the **Work Culture Notes** sections, students discuss valuable information about how to function and adapt to workplace settings. Each chapter ends with an **Assessment Activity.** A sample **Job Application** found on pages 121–122 offers students opportunities to practice filling out and checking the form with their teachers and classmates.

In the text, the SCANS (Secretary's Commission of Achieving Necessary Success) Basic and Foundation Skills from the U.S. Department of Labor are contextualized into information about the workplace. Competencies identified by CASAS (Comprehensive Adult Student Assessment System) Life Skill Competencies, are built into every chapter. A correlation of Section 4 of the CASAS Competencies (Employment Competencies) and the SCANS are shown in the chart on pages vi–vii.

*Working It Out* was written to empower students to participate fully in today's workplace with all of its changing technology, structure, and patterns of daily interaction. The components of each chapter allow students to listen to, question, discuss, evaluate, read, write, and thoroughly investigate all aspects of work. Students share the need to adapt to the workplace and acquire its language and practice.

The following are suggestions for using and enhancing the book's activities. Included are individual, pair, team, and whole class activities.

▶ **Talking About Work** Students are introduced to the theme of each chapter through class discussion of a picture. Questions engage students in lively topics such as: *Looking for a Job: Do some jobs require more English than others?* or *Technology: How do you think computers affect workers?* These discussions activate prior vocabulary and knowledge from students' life experiences, and encourage students to voice their opinions. Simultaneously, new vocabulary is introduced.

### Extension Activities

- Working in small groups, students ask and answer questions. Student A asks Student B question #1. Student B answers. Student B asks Student C question #1. Student C answers. The same question is asked to all group members. The same procedure is used for all remaining questions.
- The first picture is revisited prior to the reading the second student story in the chapter. The second story's theme is introduced through the context of the beginning picture.
- After class discussion, each student is asked to write a story about the picture.
- After discussing a question posed by the teacher, small groups of students discuss the picture, write a script, and then, act out a situation in front of the class.

▶ **Keywords** Specially chosen words introduce the main concepts of the reading. Students brainstorm word associations from key words. The teacher records the word associations on the board.

### Extension Activities

- Students make their own flash cards. Learners review the word meanings with partners.
- On the flash card students list the correct part of speech: noun, verb, adjective, etc.

▶ **Reading Strategies** Learners preview, predict, and scan stories prior to the reading. They learn to look at story components: title, picture, key words, sentences, and paragraphs. They activate background knowledge by predicting answers to questions, checking later to see if their predictions were correct. The teacher introduces key words and vocabulary words into the discussion.

### Extension Activities

- Learners look only at the photo and guess what the story is about.
- Learners are told only what the chapter title is, e.g., "*Safety.*" They are asked to tell what kind of story they would like to read on the subject of safety.

▶ **The Reading** The authentic readings introduce and reinforce the unit themes and new vocabulary words in real-life contexts. Students read the story and circle new vocabulary. New vocabulary words are discussed after each paragraph or after the entire story is completed.

### Extension Activities

- Students sit in small groups. They are each assigned a paragraph to read silently. (Student A reads paragraph #1, Student B reads paragraph #2.) After learners are finished reading their paragraphs, they report on their paragraphs to the group. Student A says, "Paragraph #1 is about . . ." Then, Student B reports on paragraph #2.
- Students sit in small groups. They offer their opinions about the issues raised in the story.

*Example:* In Chapter 1 after reading, "*How I Finally Got a Job,*" by Liliana Fialos, students discuss whether they agree with her idea of how to be successful in a job interview.

▶ **Thinking About the Story** Comprehension checks after the story allow learners to review the material, vocabulary words, and key concepts.

### Extension Activities

1. • Students sit in a team and cut out magazine pictures relating to vocabulary words or the general story theme.
   - They glue the pictures onto sheets of construction paper forming a collage.
   - The team titles the collage.
   - Each student writes four or five sentences about the collage.

- The team shares the collage with the class and a few team members read their sentences.

2. • Each student cuts out a picture of a person, a workplace, and a job (e.g., a housewife, a kitchen, and some cut vegetables).
   - They pass the three pictures to another student.
   - The second student writes a story about the person, the workplace, and the job. The story can be related to the unit theme (e.g., the work schedule and paycheck of a housewife). Pictures may be saved and recycled for future lessons.

▶ **Work Dictionary and Vocabulary Database** Students create a working dictionary in their notebooks or a vocabulary database in their computers to contain each word, meaning, and a sentence using the word. They review vocabulary words at the end of each chapter.

**Vocabulary Extension** Students team with others who have similar job experiences and talk about their specific on-the-job needs for *vocabulary* and *idioms*. Team members meet with their teacher and explain their needs. The teacher develops lessons incorporating specific vocabulary as requested by the students.

▶ **Teamwork** Cooperative team activities in the text reflect the work world in which employees work in teams to produce a product, compare life experiences, knowledge, and ideas. Teams provide supportive environments in which learners negotiate, resolve conflicts, solve problems, and come to conclusions. Teams of three or four students provide optimal participation and sharing of tasks.

*Example:* In Chapter 1, "*Looking for and Finding a Job,*" the homework assignment asks students to make a neighborhood business survey. The class is divided into teams assigned to specific neighborhood sections. Members compile lists of several businesses, the types of business, the numbers of employees, and if any new employees are needed. Teammates gather the information, report findings to the team, tabulate, chart, and present the findings to their class. Class members take notes on each presentation. The teacher checks their notes for accuracy. Team lists are compiled into a job hunting reference manual.

▶ **Work Culture Notes** These notes familiarize the learner with how workers are expected to act on-the-job, and the laws that protect workers so learners can avoid making on-the-job mistakes.

**Extension** After reading the WCN in Chapter 5, "*Communication Between a Worker and a Boss,*" each learner takes a self inventory.

*Example:* "Do I use polite English when I am talking?"

After doing a self inventory, Student A reports to Student B on his or her plans to improve on personal weak points.

▶ **Information Gathering** Students are stimulated to communicate beliefs and opinions, experiences, and values to classmates.

**Personal or Pair Inventories** Learners summarize their own information and compare their experiences.

**Team** and **Class Surveys** Experiences of group members are recorded and reported within the team, and whole class. Totals and class percentages of differences can be tabulated on the board.

**Extension** For each chapter, teachers can develop homework assignments for teams of students to report back on. Chapter 8, "*Labor Unions . . .,*" learners survey five neighbors to discover if they are union members, the name and local number of their unions, and when the unions meet. Team members chart their information and report back to their class.

▶ **Timelines** The timelines provided can be used by the student to list, order, and evaluate chronological time.

**Extension** Learners make a timeline of events in their families: births, special celebrations, deaths, moving to the United States.

★ ★ ★**Challenge Activities** Higher intermediate level activities are marked with an asterisk (★) within each chapter.

▶ **Graphs, Charts, and Workplace Documents** Learners read, interpret, and respond to work orders, forms, written procedures, memos, graphs, and charts in the workplace.

**Extension Activities**
- Learners draw organizational charts of the companies they work for including titles and departments.

- Learners brainstorm lists of all safety rules they follow at home. (see Chapter 7, *"Safety"*). Then, they prioritize their lists in order of importance and tabulate the results on a line graph.

For additional workplace statistics, refer to the *Statistical Abstract of the United States,* and the *Occupational Outlook Handbook.*

▶ **Writing Activities** Learners fill out job applications, charts, and injury forms, write memos, business letters, and requests for information. Students develop their writing using process writing techniques. At the end of the book there is a two-page job application form for student practice.

▶ **Listening Activities** The audiocassette provides learners with classroom opportunities to listen and respond to the voices of native and non-native speakers in workplace contexts. The **Listening Script** included at the back of the text allows students to check their listening comprehension and provides for additional practice.

▶ **Grammar Focus** and **Grammar Appendix** Students have the opportunity for additional practice of the language structure highlighted in each chapter in the **Grammar Appendix** activities at the back of the book.

▶ **Assessing Your Progress** Questions at the end of each chapter focus the learners back on the factual content material and cultural nuances covered in each lesson. They assess students' knowledge and indicate where review is necessary.

- Assessment questions can be modified and used by teachers as pretests.
- Learners can be asked appropriate questions from the assessments after completing sections of the chapter.

▶ **Looking Back** Learners reflect on and begin taking responsibility for what they learned in the lesson about work, about their lives, and about new vocabulary and idioms.

▶ **Computer Activities** Computer activities provide learners with opportunities to review, organize, and recycle the content of each lesson and its vocabulary words.

- *Graphs and Charts* Learners use spreadsheet or data base software to make class and team charts and graphs.
- *Letters* Students e-mail or send letters to request information, thank business and union representatives, librarians, department heads, and supervisors for assistance. They contact government officials about working conditions and how to report labor law violations.
- Students use the on-line information at the library or at home to find out about companies they are interested in working for and about labor unions.
- *Job Database* Students select particular types of jobs and make databases of local companies, the kinds of jobs available, the wages and salaries, and the experience and education required.
- *Internet and E-Mail* Students electronically connect with other students to find out how it feels to live and work in a new country.
- *Grammar and Spelling* Learners use computerized grammar and spell checkers to edit and revise their writing.
- *Publishing* Copies of student writings are printed and shared in class, with other classes, in school newspapers, and with administrators. Students use e-mail to share writing with learners at other schools.

The author and publisher would like to acknowledge the contributions of the following individuals to *Working it Out*.

Reviewers:

Sheila Acevedo, School District of Palm Beach County (West Palm Beach, FL)

Myra K. Baum, New York City Board of Education (New York, NY)

Margaret Boyter-Escalona, Chicago Teachers' Center - Northeastern Illinois (Chicago, IL)

Susan Escobar, ESL Teacher (Clovis, CA)

Myra Fernandez, Roosevelt Adult Education (Los Angeles, CA)

Marty Furch, Palomar Community College (San Marcos, CA)

Jill E. Gluck, Hollywood C.A.S. - LAUSD (Los Angeles, CA)

Pat Mooney Gonzalez, New York State Department of Education (Albany, NY)

Giang Hoang, Evans C.A.S., LAUSD (Los Angeles, CA)

Angela Locke, Santa Barbara City College (Santa Barbara, CA)

Paolo Madrigal, Mt. San Antonio College (Walnut, CA)

Jo McEntire, Shoreline Community College (Seattle, WA)

Sue E. Mendizza, Rancho Santiago College and Saddleback Community College (Trabuco Canyon, CA)

Linda Milazzo, WESL Director, - LAUSD (Los Angeles, CA)

Jean Owensby, Refugee Employment Training Project, LAUSD (Los Angeles, CA)

Andrea Paralla, Jamaica Plain Community Center at English High (Jamaica Plain, MA)

Linda Scambray, Clovis Adult School (Clovis, CA)

Kathleen Santopietro Weddell, Adult Education Consultant (Longmont, CO)

Diana Satin, Jamaica Plain Community Center at English High (Jamaica Plain, MA)

Jerry Strei, (Plantation, FL)

The following individuals made thoughtful contributions to the work as it developed:

Inez Aidlin, Steve Barba, Cliff de Cordoba, Barbara Hughes, Dan Hutchinson, Maria Kahler, Sylvia Parsley, South Gate Community Adult School, LAUSD

Eva Bol, Ph.D., Linda Roberts, Ph.D., Joan Smiles, Attorney-at-Law, Yolanda Rios Verdugo

Pat Burns, Yvonne Nishio, Evans Community Adult School, LAUSD

Marcia Chan, San Francisco Community College

Beth Easter, Minneapolis Public Schools Adult Literacy Program

George Hildebrand, Laurie Pincus, Central Adult High School, LAUSD

Mary Hurst, Dale McIntire, Nancy Woodrum, Los Angeles Community Adult School, LAUSD

Gwen Mayer, El Camino Real Community Adult School, LAUSD

Federico Marquez Palacios

Roberta Medford, UCLA Library

Terry Lynn Padilla, Public Relations Officer, Department of Veteran's Affairs

Mim Paggi, Franklin Community Adult School, LAUSD

Shannon Reininger, Safety/Environmental Coordinator, AHF Ducommon, Gandena, CA

Lynne Suio, Gardena Community Adult School, LAUSD

**Acknowledgements**

Many special thanks go to Sally Conover, Associate Developmental Editor, for her persistence and dedication. She provided a knowledge of adult ESL, professionalism, and continuity to *Working It Out*. Thank you to Mike Burggren, Production Services Coordinator at Heinle and Heinle, who provided thoughtfulness, caring, and great insight. Mike's earnest persistence brought the book to a happy completion. Thanks to Jonathan Boggs, Market Development Director, who gave the planning and follow through on *Working It Out* humor, vision, depth, and wisdom. Thanks to Roseanne Mendoza, editor, for her commitment to quality work. She, from the book's inception, understood and pushed for vocational ESL materials that met the highest standards. Thanks to Amy Lawler, Managing Developmental Editor, for her awareness of the significance of workplace materials in the adult ESL classroom and for thoughtfully overseeing this project.

Ronna Magy

# 1 LOOKING FOR AND FINDING A JOB

## 1. Talking About Finding Work

▲ **Look at the picture. Discuss these questions with your teacher and class.**

    ▶ What is happening in the picture?
    ▶ What are some other ways to look for a job in the United States?
    ▶ Who can help you find a job?
    ▶ Do some jobs require more English than others? Which ones?
  ★ ▶ What do you need to bring with you when you apply for a job?
  ★ ▶ Is finding a job in the United States easier or more difficult than finding a job in your country? Why?

1

## 2. Work Stories

**A** Discuss the words with your teacher and classmates. Write your ideas on the lines.

finding a job    keeping a job

**B** Read

▲ Liliana Fialos

### Reading Strategy: Look and Predict
Before you read the story, look at the title. Look at the pictures on this page and the previous page. What do you think the story is about? Talk about it with your class.

**How I Finally Found a Job** by Liliana Fialos

There's nothing more exciting than looking for a job. It's a long process of reading ads and making telephone calls. The hardest part of the process is the job interview.

In my country, Honduras, the **job search** is easier. Very often, you get a job using **"pull"** or through **"connections."** As a result, the interview is not formal.

The employment ritual in the United States requires behavior that goes against my training. In American culture you have to be **direct** in your answers. Job applicants are expected to be **assertive,** since this is an important value in this culture. This makes me feel I am not **modest.** In my culture you discuss your skills **indirectly,** in a diplomatic way. Otherwise, you are considered arrogant.

This cultural confusion cost me my first two jobs. First I applied for a clerical job answering the telephone and filing.

**Definitions**

**job search** looking for a job

**pull** to have power and influence

**connections** a relationship where one person does favors for another

**direct** open and honest

**assertive** confident, aggressive

**modest** a person who does not talk about himself or herself a lot

**indirectly** not directly

When the interviewer asked about my previous experience, I didn't say anything. I thought saying nothing would help me get the job. But I didn't! My second job interview was for selling clothes. They asked me, "Do you have experience in sales?" I said, "No, but I can learn." Unfortunately, they wanted someone with experience.

Once I understood what was expected, I became more assertive. In the third interview, I was **successful.** When they asked about my selling experience I told them, "I don't have experience selling, but I have a lot of experience buying! I know how customers like to be treated and I love to help customers find what they want." They hired me immediately!

## 3. Thinking about the Story

**A** Talk about these questions with a partner.

1. Name two ways Liliana suggests looking for a job.

2. Why does she say to be direct during a job interview in the United States?

3. How do people get jobs in Honduras?

4. What made Liliana successful in the third job interview?

★ 5. What do you think are the best ways to find a job?

**B** Read Liliana's story again. Work with a partner. Compare how a job interview in your culture is the same or different from a job interview in the United States. Write your answers.

| | UNITED STATES | MY NATIVE COUNTRY |
|---|---|---|
| **1.** What clothes should you wear? | | |
| **2.** What time should you arrive? | | |
| **3.** What things should you discuss? | | |
| **4.** What things shouldn't you discuss? | | |
| **5.** Should you smile, laugh, or be serious? | | |
| **6.** Should you make eye contact? | | |
| **7.** Other | | |

**C** Share your information. Your teacher will ask students to compare job interviews in their countries with job interviews in the United States.

★ **D** Sit with a partner who has had a job interview. Talk about what he or she liked or didn't like about the interview. What can you learn from the interview? Now write a paragraph about the interview. Then read it to another classmate.

**E** Read the story again. Circle any new words. Begin a **work dictionary** in your notebook or a vocabulary database in your computer. Write the meanings next to the words. Use the words in a sentence.

| Word | Meaning | Sentence |
|------|---------|----------|
| *successful* | not a failure | Her job search was successful. She got the job. |

## 4. After the Story

**A** With your teacher and classmates, make a list of all the jobs students in your class have or would like to have. Write the list on the chalkboard.

**B** Think about looking for a job. Listen as your teacher reads the questions. Write your answers.

**1.** What job would you like to have? _____

**2.** What are some things you look for in a job?

_____

_____

**C** Read these two job ads from the classified section of the newspaper. Answer the questions.

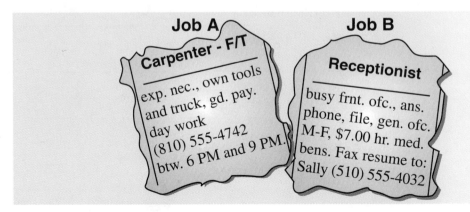

**Job A**

**Carpenter - F/T**

exp. nec., own tools and truck, gd. pay. day work
(810) 555-4742
btw. 6 PM and 9 PM.

**Job B**

**Receptionist**

busy frnt. ofc., ans. phone, file, gen. ofc. M-F, $7.00 hr. med. bens. Fax resume to:
Sally (510) 555-4032

| | Job A | Job B |
|---|---|---|
| What is the job? | | |
| How much does it pay? | | |
| What are the benefits? | | |
| What are the hours? | | |
| What **skills** and experience are necessary for the job? | | |
| Who should you call or write? | | |
| What is the phone number or address? | | |

**D** Bring in a newspaper ad for a job that interests you. Read the ad. Present it to your class. Explain why it interests you.

> *Example:* This ad is for a job as a *nurse*.
> I like the *hours and the benefits of this job.*
> I'd like to have this job because *it is near my home and with a good hospital.*

**E** A nurse's assistant is applying for a job. Read the sample letter below. Use the letter as a model. Write a letter to a company that explains the job you are looking for and your experience. If possible, type the letter on your word processing program.

6957 Forest Avenue
Detroit, Michigan 48221
April 2, 1997

John Pavlick, Personnel Director
Montgomery Hospital
1439 South Elm Street
Detroit, Michigan 48221

Dear Mr. Pavlick:

　　I am interested in applying for the job as a nurse's assistant in your hospital. I have four years' experience working as a nurse's assistant in the United States. In my country I studied nursing at National Nursing School.

　　I am a serious and responsible worker. I come to work on time and make sure all my work is done well. I give my patients excellent care.

　　I look forward to meeting you. I would like to set up a time for an interview. Please contact me at (810) 555-3232.

Sincerely yours,

*Champa Patel*

Champa Patel

# 5. Inventory: Job Priorities, Personal Qualities

**A** Compile a class list of characteristics to look for in a job. Your teacher will write the list on the board. Copy the list.

**B** Pay, full-time hours, location, benefits, and shift are five **factors** workers say are important in selecting a job. Select the factor that is the most important to you. Tell why it is the most important factor. Your teacher will survey the class and write the totals on the board. Together, make a bar graph from your class information.

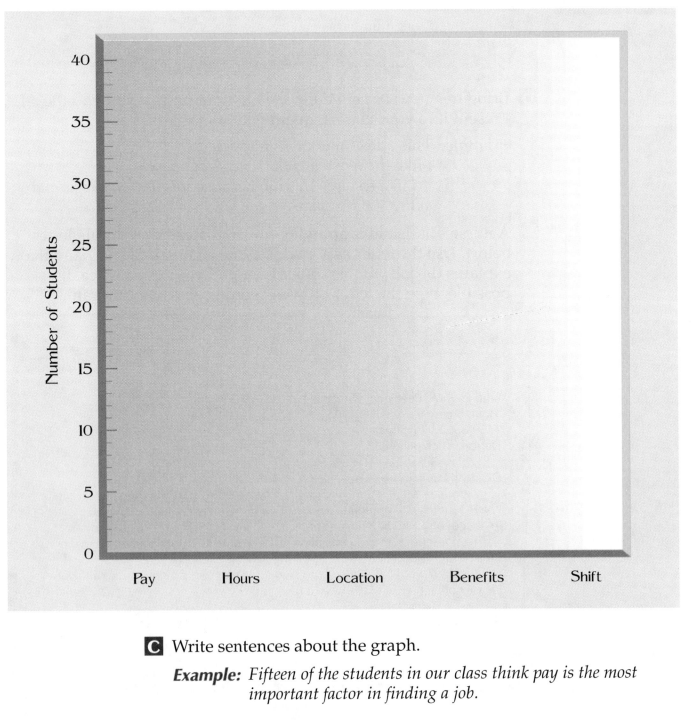

**C** Write sentences about the graph.

**Example:** *Fifteen of the students in our class think pay is the most important factor in finding a job.*

## D Work Culture Notes: Personality

Employers look for specific qualities in a new employee. You, the applicant, need to **"put your best foot forward"**. You will need to talk about your positive qualities in the job interview using some of the words below.

| | | |
|---|---|---|
| friendly | cooperative | dependable, reliable, responsible |
| organized | serious | **team player** |
| flexible | efficient | good communicator |
| hardworking | fast learner | **gets along with** others |
| patient | intelligent | uses **common sense** |
| honest | good listener | follows instructions |
| punctual | | |

For more help with **adjectives,** turn to the **Grammar Appendix.**

### Definitions

**put your best foot forward** describe yourself in the best possible way

**team player** person who works well with others

**get along well** have a friendly relationship

**common sense** good judgment; to understand something from your life experience

**E** Circle the qualities in D that describe your personality. Work with a partner. Practice talking about your positive qualities. Student A is the interviewer. Student B is the job applicant.

**Example:**

Interviewer: *What can you tell me about yourself?*
Applicant: *I am serious and responsible.*
*I get along well with others.*
*I like working in a team.*

Now make an X next to some areas that you need to improve.

 **F** Sit in a group. Read Liliana's story again. Why do you think it is important to be confident and positive in a job interview? Each person has two minutes to explain.

# 6. Second Story: The Job Interview

**A** Read the story.

▲ Avelina Jose

**My Job Interview** by Avelina Jose

My friend Cirvilla worked at a fast-food restaurant for five years. When the manager needed a new cook, Cirvilla suggested he call me for a job interview.

When I went to the restaurant, the manager asked a lot of questions. He asked, "Have you ever worked before? Do you have any experience as a cook or cashier? How much money do you want to earn? What hours can you work?" There were many questions and I was very nervous!

I got the job! I was very surprised and I felt very happy! After the interview the manager said, "I will call you to come back next week for two hours of training." He also gave me a uniform.

I was trained to prepare different kinds of hamburgers. Later, I was trained to wait on customers. It was a good experience for me to work there. I learned a lot. I had to stop working after my child was born.

**B** Talk about these questions in a group.

1. How did Avelina find out about the job?
2. How did she feel during the job interview?
3. How many different jobs did she have at the restaurant?
★ 4. How would you have answered the questions in the second paragraph?

# 7. Job Interview Questions and Answers

**A** In a group, brainstorm eight questions an employer asks in a job interview. Cover these topics: past work experience, education, personal qualities, and job skills. Share your list with your class.

*Examples:* Tell me about your experience in *electronics.*
What did you do *on your last job?*
Have you ever used *a computer?*

_____

_____

_____

_____

_____

**B** With your teammates, list five questions an applicant can ask in a job interview. Include salary, hours, benefits, overtime, and training. Share the list with your class.

**Examples:** Are there *medical benefits?*
Is there *overtime pay?*

_____

_____

_____

_____

_____

**C** Choose a partner. Practice answering the applicant's questions. Then choose another partner and practice again.

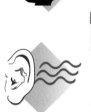

**D** Listen to the questions and circle the correct responses.

1. **a.** The Personnel Office is on your right.
   **b.** Auto body repair person.
   **c.** I did maintenance work in my country.

2. **a.** I was employed as a dental hygienist.
   **b.** Gardening is my hobby.
   **c.** My sister worked in the main office.

3. **a.** I worked as a carpenter for seven years.
   **b.** I moved to the United States five years ago.
   **c.** I want to be a computer operator.

4. **a.** I have two children.
   **b.** Third shift is best for me.
   **c.** I'm hardworking and honest.

5. **a.** I can cook and clean, and I'm good at taking care of children.
   **b.** I have a car.
   **c.** I can work any shift.

6. **a.** I can operate a computer.
   **b.** I would prefer to work day shift during the week.
   **c.** My children are in school.

# 8. Working with Forms: The Job Application

**A** Imagine you are applying for a job. Look at the sample job application below.

**Personal Information**

| Name: | Last | First | Middle | Home Phone |
|---|---|---|---|---|
| | Suio | Mark | M. | (213) 555-7128 |

| Address | Work Phone |
|---|---|
| 12976 East Spaulding Avenue | |

| City | State | Zip | Social Security Number |
|---|---|---|---|
| Los Angeles | CA | 90026 | 427-91-2396 |

**Work History**

| Company | Phone Number |
|---|---|
| North Hospital | (310) 555-7190 |

| Address, City, State, Zip Code | Employment Dates |
|---|---|
| 3945 Century Park North | |
| Los Angeles, CA 90001 | 3/93–1/95 |

| Job Title | Supervisor | Salary |
|---|---|---|
| Custodian | Stan Stevens | $7.00 per hour |

**B** Complete these sections of the job application form for yourself. Print clearly.

**Personal Information**

| Name: | Last | First | Middle | Home Phone |
|---|---|---|---|---|
| | | | | |

| Address | Work Phone |
|---|---|
| | |

| City | State | Zip | Social Security Number |
|---|---|---|---|
| | | | |

**Work History**

| Company | Phone Number |
|---|---|
| | |

| Address, City, State, Zip Code | Employment Dates |
|---|---|
| | |

| Job Title | Supervisor | Salary |
|---|---|---|
| | | |

**C** Ask a classmate to check your application form and sign his or her initials below if the information is filled in correctly.

All information is printed clearly. _____

All information is filled in completely. _____

**D** Below are additional questions you may be asked on a job application or in an interview. Practice asking and answering the questions with a partner.

**1.** Do you have the legal right to work in this country?

**2.** Are you over the age of 18?

**3.** Where are you working now?

**4.** What is your present supervisor's name?

**5.** Can we contact your present employer?

**6.** Have you or has anyone in your family worked for this company?

**E** Complete this section of the job application form using your information.

Do you have a work permit? _____

Are you 18 or older? _____

Where are you working now? _____

Can we contact your present employer? _____

Have you or has anyone in your family ever worked for this company?

_____

★ **F** Gather additional job application forms from employers in your neighborhood. Practice filling out the forms, checking the forms, and interviewing student applicants. Invite an employer to visit your class and explain what he or she looks for in a job applicant.

## 9. Situations

**A** Four applicants apply for a job as a city bus driver. You and your teammates are the employers. Consider each applicant's qualifications and information.

**Applicant A** is a 30-year-old female with three years of experience as a bus driver. She has no history of accidents or safety violations. She lives 20 miles from her job. She is very serious about doing a good job.

**Applicant B** is a 50-year-old male. He has twenty years of experience as a truck driver. On his previous job there was an accident with his truck, but he was not responsible. He likes to work with people. His last supervisor did not recommend him because he has a bad temper.

**Applicant C** is a 27-year-old male. He has four years of experience driving a school bus. He is the son of the company vice president. When he was 16, he was arrested for drunk driving. He says he is more serious now.

**Applicant D** is a 40-year-old female. She drove a taxi in her country for ten years. She has five parking tickets, but no accidents. She lives near the bus company.

**B** Record each applicant's information on the form below.

| NAME | YEARS OF EXPERIENCE | OTHER INFORMATION |
|---|---|---|
|  |  |  |
|  |  |  |
|  |  |  |

**C** Discuss each applicant's information with your teammates. Come to a team decision on who you would hire and why. Compare your decision to those of other groups.

# 10. What We Say at Work

**A** Listen to the job interviews. Circle if the applicant's answer is **Yes** or **No**.

| | | |
|---|---|---|
| **1.** | Yes | No |
| **2.** | Yes | No |
| **3.** | Yes | No |
| **4.** | Yes | No |
| **5.** | Yes | No |

# 11. Workplace Vocabulary

| | | |
|---|---|---|
| direct | job application | team players |
| gets along with | searched | put your best foot forward |
| indirectly | job interview | priority |

**A** Fill in the following sentences using the workplace vocabulary. Compare your answers with your classmates. Then find the pages where the words are used and write the page numbers. Compare the sentences you found with the sentences on this page.

**Page Number**

1. If you are looking for a job in the United States, give _____ answers in a job interview. _____

2. In Honduras, where Liliana is from, people speak more _____ in a job interview. _____

3. The form you fill out when looking for a job is the _____ _____. _____

4. Keiko had a _____ _____ with the personnel supervisor at the post office. _____

5. Kim has a good relationship with her coworkers; she _____ _____ _____ others. _____

6. All the employees worked together. Anna took the orders, Olga got the products from the warehouse, and Tim sent the orders to the customers. They were _____ _____. _____

7. When you talk about your positive qualities in a job interview, you _____ _____ _____ _____ _____. _____

8. Yael _____ for a job for several months. _____

9. Reiko needed to find a job that was close to her home. It was her number one _____. _____

**B** Select two words from the vocabulary list. Write each word on a piece of paper. Ask one student to give a definition of one word and to use the word in a sentence. Then ask another student to define the second word and use it in a sentence.

*Examples:* *Question:* What does **gets along with** mean?
*Answer:* It means to be friendly with other people.
*Question:* Please use **gets along with** in a sentence.
*Answer:* Sayeed gets along well with his classmates.

# 12. Assessment

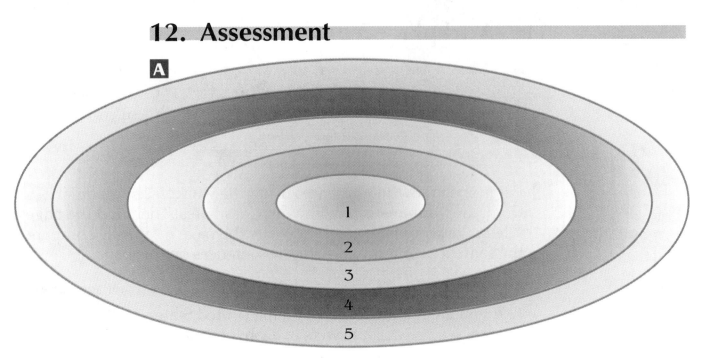

1. In space 1, write the job you want to have.
2. In space 2, list five of your best personal qualities.
3. In space 3, list your job priorities (pay, benefits, location, hours).
4. In space 4, list your work skills (things you can do).
5. In space 5, write five possible places you could find a job.

# 13. Looking Back

| A Things I learned about looking for and finding a job | How I can apply what I learned to my life |
|---|---|
| 1. | |
| 2. | |
| 3. | |
| B New words and idioms from the unit | Related words from my job |
| 1. | |
| 2. | |
| 3. | |

# 2 STARTING A NEW JOB

## 1. Talking About Work

▲ **Look at the picture. Discuss these questions with your teacher and class.**

| Definition | |
|---|---|
| **experienced** someone who has done something before | ▶ What is happening in the picture? |
| | ▶ Is the new waitress having an easy first day? |
| | ▶ Do the **experienced** workers want to help the new worker? |
| | ★ ▶ If you were the new waitress, what help would you want from the manager? from the other waitresses? |
| | ★ ▶ In general, does a customer get the same service from a new worker as from an experienced worker? |

# 2. Work Stories

**A** Discuss the words with your teacher and classmates. Write your ideas on the lines.

```
_____                    _____
                   } first day of work {
_____                    _____
```

**B** Read

▲ Michiko Heald

## Reading Strategy: Read and Predict

Before you read the story, look at the title. Read the first and last sentences of each paragraph. What do you think the story is about?

## My First Day
## Selling Clothes by Michiko Heald

I woke up early on my first day of work. I was a little nervous. I had to go to work at the Base Exchange at the Los Angeles Air Force Station. It was 1981. First I went to the Personnel Office, and I was introduced to the supervisor of the Ladies Clothing Department. I was happy about working there. I thought I would have the first chance to buy whatever I wanted.

As soon as the doors opened, the customers came in and I had to help them all day long. The customers tried on the clothes. When the customers asked me, I gave them my opinion about the clothes. I had two **coworkers**. They only talked to me a little that day. The supervisor was watching every move I made. At the end of the day, the supervisor told me that my work was excellent. She liked me, and I was happy.

When I got home, I was exhausted. I told my husband to get some take-out food that night. He asked me, "Didn't you buy any clothes for yourself today?" Then he smiled. I was too tired to answer his joke. I think everyone will be **exhausted** mentally and physically after his or her first day of work.

## Definitions

**coworker** someone you work with

**exhausted** very tired

# 3. Thinking About the Story

**A** Talk about these questions with a partner.

1. Where was Michiko's job?
2. What did she do on that job?
★ 3. Was her first day of work what she expected?
★ 4. What are some things workers need to adjust to on a new job?
★ 5. What are some things to think about and learn before your first day on a new job?

**B** Read Michiko's story again. With a classmate, write four additional *wh* questions asking who, what, where, when, why, or how about her story.

_____

_____

_____

_____

_____

_____

**C** Work in a group of four. Ask the group members your questions about the story. Then answer their questions about the story. (Don't look back at the story.)

**D** Read the story again. Circle any new words. Add these words to the **work dictionary** in your notebook or to the vocabulary database in your computer. Write the meaning next to each word. Use it in a sentence.

| Word | Meaning | Sentence |
|------|---------|----------|
| *coworker* | someone you work with | I get along well with my coworkers. |

# 4. After the Story

**A** Think about your first day on a job. (If you have never worked, think about the job of someone you know.) Your teacher will read the questions. Write your answers. Then ask a classmate the questions. Listen and write his or her answers.

| First Day on the Job | You | Your Classmate |
|---|---|---|
| 1. Where did you work? | | |
| 2. What was your job? | | |
| 3. Did you arrive early, on time, or late? | | |
| 4. Was the supervisor friendly or unfriendly? | | |
| 5. Did the other workers talk to you? | | |
| 6. Did the other workers sit with you at break time and lunch time? | | |
| 7. How did you feel before you started working? | | |
| 8. How did you feel at the end of the day? | | |

**B** In a group, discuss the following questions. One student can be the recorder and writes down the group responses.

   1. Did you and your classmates have similar experiences on your first day of work?

   2. Do you think a first day of work is easier for older workers or for younger workers? Why? for men or for women? Why?

  ★ 3. What can you do to feel more comfortable on the first day of your next job?

  ★ 4. What can you do or say to help a new worker feel comfortable on a new job?

  ★ 5. How can what you do or say on your first day of work help or hurt you on the job?

**C** After all the questions are asked and answered, your group's recorder will report the answers to the class.

Compare the answers of the groups. Discuss similarities and differences.

 **D** Cut out pictures of people working at different jobs from magazines or newspapers and bring them to class. Talk about the people, the work they are doing, and how you think they felt on their first day on the job. What are some problems they had?

 ★ **E** Select one of the pictures from D. Write a story about the person and the job. When you are finished, do a spell check on a word processing program or ask a partner to check your spelling.

## 5. Inventory

**A** **Work Culture Notes: Making Contact, Making Friends**

To get to know your coworkers you can:

1. Smile and say hello when you arrive at work.

2. Look into the eyes of another person when you are talking with him or her (make eye contact).

| Definition |
|---|
| **positive attitude** optimistic, hopeful |

3. Speak slowly and clearly.

4. Have a **positive attitude** about work.

5. Work together with coworkers in teams. Talk about your work.

6. Ask for help with work problems. If you don't understand some instructions, ask a coworker to explain them to you.

7. Sit with other workers at break time and lunch time. Listen to what others talk about. Make small talk. Let people get to know you. Bring in photos of your family or country.

8. Share food from your country with coworkers. Talk about similarities and differences between your country and the United States.

9. Say goodbye when you leave.

**B** To do the things suggested in 5A you will need to practice your English as much as possible. Think of some ways to do that with your classmates.

*Example:* Practice using English with family members, neighbors, and workers in local businesses.

**C** When you start a new job, it's important to make a good impression. What will help you make a good impression? What will make a bad impression? Make a check (✔) under good impression or bad impression. Talk about your answers with the class.

|  | GOOD IMPRESSION | BAD IMPRESSION |
|---|---|---|
| 1. Looking down, not looking at anyone |  |  |
| 2. Talking about problems you had on your last job |  |  |
| 3. Smiling and making eye contact with others |  |  |
| 4. Not talking |  |  |
| 5. Dressing neatly |  |  |
| 6. Frequently coming to work late |  |  |
| 7. Asking questions if you don't understand |  |  |
| 8. Follow directions |  |  |
| 9. Only talking to others from your country |  |  |
| 10. Disagreeing with the boss |  |  |

# 6. Preparing for the First Day at Work

**A** Read the story.

▲ Ryu Seoung Whoon

**Going to Work My First Day** by Ryu Seoung Whoon

I'll never forget my first day of work. I got up very early. I dressed carefully. Then I ate breakfast.

I left my home at 7:30 A.M. I was supposed to start work at 9:00 A.M. It took about one hour from my house to the new company. I left home 30 minutes earlier than necessary so I could beat the traffic.

When I arrived at the company, I didn't know what time it was. I didn't see any other employees. I waited and waited. They arrived one hour after me! Later I found out why. My wife had set our clock one hour early! I arrived at work at 7:30 A.M., instead of 8:30 A.M. I laughed about that to myself.

Because I was so early my coworkers called me "the eager beaver." After that first early arrival, I always got to work first, before my other coworkers.

**B** Answer these questions in a group. Write down your answers.

1. How did Ryu Seoung Whoon prepare for his first day at work?

   a. *He got up at 5:00 A.M.* _____

   b. _____

   c. _____

2. How did his wife try to help him?

   _____

3. Why did his coworkers give him the **nickname** "eager beaver"?

   _____

**C** Think about your first day on a job or your first day in class. How did you prepare for it? Were there any problems? Write about this for five minutes. Read what you wrote to a partner. Then listen to your partner's story.

## 7. Situations

**A** At a new job your coworkers will want to know about you. Talk to your teacher and your class about the following questions. Which do you think are appropriate to ask a new worker? Which are inappropriate? Why?

| | APPROPRIATE | INAPPROPRIATE |
|---|---|---|
| 1. What's your name? | | |
| 2. What country are you from? | | |
| 3. Where do you live now? | | |
| 4. Are you married? | | |
| 5. Do you have a boyfriend or a girlfriend? | | |
| 6. How many children do you have? | | |
| 7. Do your children live with you in this country? | | |
| 8. How did you get this job? | | |
| 9. Did you do this kind of work before? When? Where? | | |
| 10. How much money do you make? | | |

**B** Review the questions in 7A with a partner. Identify the *wh* and *how* questions. Look at the way the questions are formed.

**C** Now imagine you are talking to a coworker. Practice asking and answering these questions with a partner.

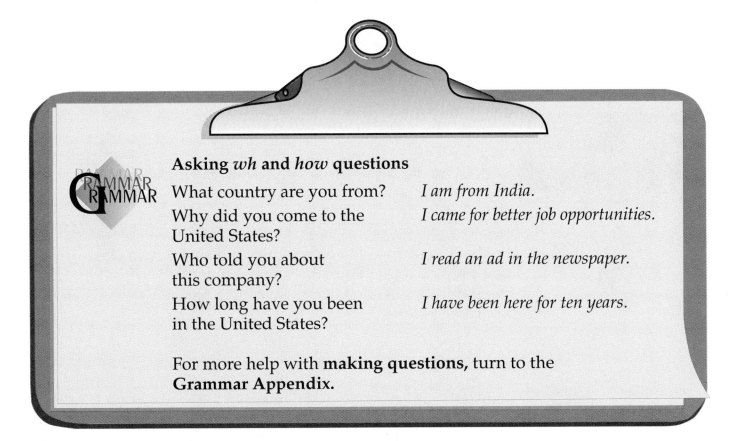

**Asking *wh* and *how* questions**

| | |
|---|---|
| What country are you from? | *I am from India.* |
| Why did you come to the United States? | *I came for better job opportunities.* |
| Who told you about this company? | *I read an ad in the newspaper.* |
| How long have you been in the United States? | *I have been here for ten years.* |

For more help with **making questions,** turn to the **Grammar Appendix.**

**D** Work in a small group. Read and act out each of the scenes.

1. You are a new teacher in an elementary school. You teach second grade. It is your first day on the job. The students talk all the time. They are not doing their lessons. The class is out of control.

   Who do you ask for advice?

   What do they tell you?

2. You work in a machine shop operating a big machine. It is your first day. There are nine other workers in your department. The boss tells you to keep the machine running. At 12 o'clock the other workers stop working and go to lunch. They tell you to come with them. The boss doesn't tell you to stop working. You don't know what to do, so you continue working.

   What do the other workers say to you when they come back from lunch?

   What do you say to them?

3. You bus tables in a large restaurant. It is your first day on the job. While you are clearing a table, you accidentally drop some water glasses on the floor and they break. The manager comes over and is very upset.

What does the manager say to you?

What do you say to the manager?

4. You are a new nurse at a hospital. Dr. Locke tells you to call the lab and order some blood and urine tests on the patient in room 9. Then the doctor leaves the hospital. You pick up the phone to call the lab. You realize Dr. Locke didn't tell you which blood and urine tests to order.

What do you do?

Who can you ask for help in this situation?

## 8. Work Memos

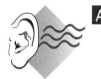 **A** Companies often call meetings for new employees. Listen to two new workers discussing a work memo. Then answer the questions.

**BEC Burns Electronics Corporation**

```
Memo to: New employees on the first shift
From: Jean Nagano, Personnel Director
Date: September 20, 1998



Orientation meeting.
Attendance is mandatory.
```

**B** Answer these questions about the memo.

1. What are the date and time of the meeting? _____

2. What is the reason for the meeting? _____

*(continued on next page)*

**3.** Is the meeting required or is it optional? _____

**4.** What information will be discussed? _____

**5.** Where will the meeting be held? _____

★ **6.** Talk with a partner. What are two specific things you think will be discussed in the meeting?

_____

_____

**C** Imagine you are Jean Nagano, Personnel Director of a large factory. What are six specific things you might talk to new employees about? Include information about work rules, safety, breaks, and restrooms.

*breaks are limited to 15 minutes*

_____

_____

_____

_____

_____

# 9. Reading a Floor Plan

**A** When you start a new job, it is important to understand where everything is. Read the company floor plan.

## ≡ITP Technics Corporation

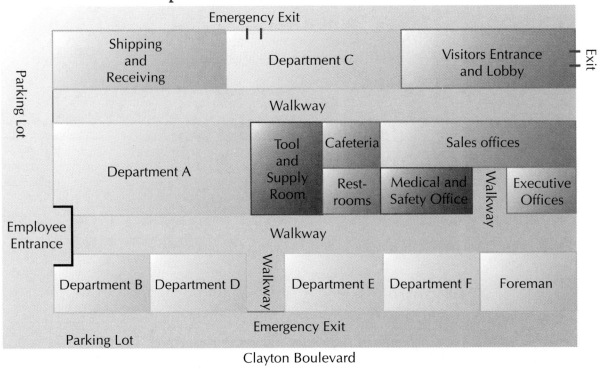

Clayton Boulevard

**B** Write short answers for the following questions. Use the prepositions *next to*, *between*, or *near* in your answers.

1. Where is the parking lot? _____

2. Where are the restrooms? _____

3. If you have a safety or a medical emergency, where would you go? _____
_____

4. Where can you get your tools repaired? _____
_____

5. Where is the cafeteria located? _____
_____

6. How many emergency exits are there? _____
Where are they located? _____
_____

 ★ **C** Draw a floor plan of the company where you work, of this school, or of your home. With a partner, ask and answer questions like those in 9B about your floor plan.

# 10. First Day of Work Issues

 **A** Listen to these questions about work. What specific information is given? Circle the appropriate answers.

1. a. near the Personnel Office
   b. near the supervisor's office

2. a. long pants, a long-sleeved shirt, goggles, and leather shoes
   b. long pants and a T-shirt

3. a. Black Tree Shoes
   b. Black Hawk Shoes

4. a. 10:00 A.M.–10:30 A.M.
   b. 10:00 A.M.–10:15 A.M.

5. a. near the cafeteria
   b. near the tool crib

# 11. Understanding Work Graphs

**Occupations Increasing in Employment 1994–2005**

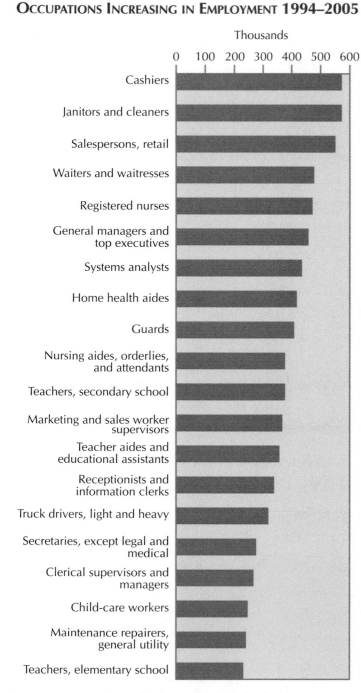

Thousands

Source: *Occupational Outlook Handbook 1996–7.*
The United States Department of Labor.

**A** Twenty occupations will increase the most in numbers between 1994 and 2005. Working as a class, study the graph. Read the information.

**B** Answer the questions about the graph.

1. What years does the graph cover? _____

2. What occupation will have the greatest increase?

   _____

3. Which are the top three occupational groups that are increasing?

   _____

   _____

4. Which three education-related occupations are listed?

   _____

   _____

5. Which three health care-related occupations are listed?

   _____

6. Of the 20 occupations, which are entry-level jobs?

   _____

7. Of the 20 occupations, which interest you?

   _____

## 12. Crossword Puzzle

**A** Fill in the words.

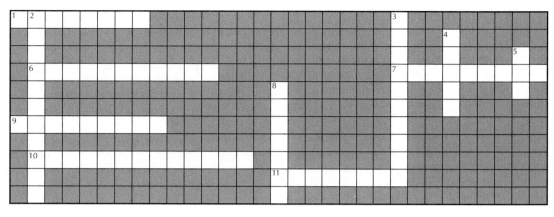

**ACROSS**

1. If you look for the good things in life, you have a _____ attitude.
6. An _____ worker is someone who has spent a lot of time on the job.
7. After the first day of work you may be mentally and physically _____.
9. A _____ meeting is a meeting you are required to attend.
10. An _____ question is too personal.
11. Someone who works in the same department as you is your _____.

**DOWN**

2. An _____ meeting gives information about a new job.
3. Another word for boss is _____.
4. When you talk to coworkers about everyday things, you are making _____ talk.
5. If this is your first day on the the job, you are a _____ worker.
8. When you meet someone for the first time, it is important to make eye _____.

## 13. Assessing Your Progress

**A** Answer the following questions.

1. Describe an experienced worker.

_____

2. Describe a good coworker.

_____

*(continued on next page)*

**3.** Name three things that make a good impression on supervisors and coworkers.

_____

_____

_____

**4.** Name three things that make a bad impression on supervisors and coworkers.

_____

_____

_____

**5.** Why is it important to have a positive attitude at work?

_____

_____

**6.** Why is attendance mandatory at a work orientation meeting?

_____

_____

**7.** Give four examples of things that are talked about in an orientation meeting.

_____     _____

_____     _____

# 14. Looking Back

| **A** Things I learned about starting a job | How I can apply what I learned to my life |
|---|---|
| **1.** | |
| **2.** | |
| **3.** | |
| **B** New words and idioms from the unit | Related words from my job |
| **1.** | |
| **2.** | |
| **3.** | |

# 3 TECHNOLOGY AND TRAINING

## 1. Talking About Work

▲ **Look at the pictures. Discuss these questions with your teacher and class.**

> ▶ Is the work in the pictures computerized?
> ▶ What skills or training do the workers need for each job?
> ★ ▶ How do you think computers will affect the workers in both pictures in the future?
> ★ ▶ How can workers prepare for new types of technology at work?

# 2. Work Stories

**A** Discuss the words with your teacher and classmates. Write your ideas on the lines.

}  technology    computers  {

**B** Read

▲ Jesus Alvarez

## Definitions

**hubcap**  metal cover over the center of a wheel

**safety glasses**  glasses to protect the eyes

**face shield**  protective covering over face

**ear plug**  rubber or wax put in ear to keep out sound

**mold**  a container into which hot liquid metal is poured and shaped

**liquid**  not solid; for example, water

**furnace**  place to melt metal at high temperature

**ladle**  large cup with long handle

### Reading Strategy: Predict

Before you read the story, quickly look at the first two paragraphs. Then talk about the questions.

1. Why do you think Jesus needs safety clothing?
2. What do you think makes his job dangerous?

Then, read the story and see if you answered correctly.

## How My Job Has Changed
by Jesus Alvarez

I started work in October 1987. At that time the company employed almost 1000 people. Our factory makes **hubcaps** for tires. The supervisor showed me around. He told me, "Here is the safety clothing you will need to wear." He gave me a pair of **safety glasses**, a **face shield**, gloves, **ear plugs**, and some safety shoes.

My work was to fill the hubcap **molds** with **liquid** aluminum. I worked near the **furnace**. The temperature of the hot aluminum was about 1300 degrees. I picked up a large **ladle** and walked with it about 30 feet. I filled the ladle with very hot liquid metal, walked back and poured the metal into the molds. I waited about two minutes. Then I went back to the first mold, opened it, took the tire rim out, and checked the rim to see if it was okay.

My coworkers and I did this work all day, every day. The temperature in the factory was very hot—about 110° Fahrenheit. It was hard physical work. In the summer, the factory air was **polluted** by chemicals. We only had two 15-minute breaks and no lunch. We worked 10 hours a day, even on Saturdays and Sundays. Sometimes we couldn't even leave our machines on our breaks. A lot of people got sick because of the heat. I used to get **cramps** in my arms and legs from **dehydration**. If anyone spilled the liquid aluminum on his body, he got a really bad burn.

The entire factory was **computerized** in 1993. Almost 500 people were laid off. Since then, **robots** do some of the dangerous work. A robot pours the liquid aluminum into the mold. My coworkers and I run the computer and remove the hot rims from the molds. We have to work as fast as the robots work and they don't ever stop! Now we work an eight-hour day with two 20-minute breaks. There is still no lunch hour. The temperature in the factory is the same, 110° Fahrenheit, but now there are fans. Workers still faint or get burned on the job, but it isn't as bad as before.

The new technology affects us in many ways. Our jobs are a little easier because robots do some of the dangerous work. But we have to know how to use computers. We have to punch many numbers into the computers and understand the codes. We don't have to work quite so hard. But I worry. Maybe in the future, they won't need people, just machines. Then where will we find jobs?

## Definitions

**pollute** to make the environment dirty

**cramp** muscle contraction and pain

**dehydration** insufficient water in the body

**computerized** changed to machines with computers

**robot** mechanical being

## 3. Thinking About the Story

**A** Work with a partner. Use information from the story to fill in the chart.

| | 1987 | 1993 |
|---|---|---|
| Number of employees in the factory | | |
| Jesus's hours of work | | |
| Jesus's job | | |
| Factory working conditions | | |

**B** Work with a different partner. Ask and answer questions from the chart in 3A.

> **Example:** Question: *How many employees worked in the factory in 1987?*
> Answer: *Almost 1000 people.*

⋆ **C** Each paragraph has a topic. Work with your partner and write what each paragraph is about.

Paragraph 1- *Jesus's new job—general information* _____

Paragraph 2- _____

Paragraph 3- _____

Paragraph 4- _____

Paragraph 5- _____

**D** Read the story again. Circle any new words. Add these words to the **work dictionary** in your notebook or to the vocabulary database in your computer. Write the meaning next to each word. Use it in a sentence.

| Word | Meaning | Sentence |
|------|---------|----------|
| *pollute* | to make something unclean | Chemicals polluted the air in the factory. |

## 4. After the Story

**A** Think about a job, the machines used on the job, and the working conditions. Your teacher will read the questions. Write your answers. If you are not sure of an answer, write "not sure." Then ask a partner the questions. Write down your partner's answers.

|  | YOU | YOUR PARTNER |
|--|-----|--------------|
| **1.** What is the job? | | |
| **2.** List the machines used on the job. | | |
| **3.** Are the machines computerized? | | |

*(continued on next page)*

**Definition**

training
education
in special
skills

| | You | Your Partner |
|---|---|---|
| **4.** What **training** do workers need to operate the machines? | | |
| **5.** Are there training classes on the job? | | |
| **6.** Were the same machines used ten years ago? | | |
| **7.** What level of English do workers need on that job (beginning, intermediate, advanced)? | | |
| **8.** Is the job safe? | | |

**B** Work with a group. Pick three of the questions from 4A. Compile the group's answers to the questions. Report the information to the class.

# 5. Education, Skills, and Training Inventory

**A** With your class, brainstorm a list of adult schools, community colleges, technical schools, and training programs nearby. Get information from your teacher, the telephone book, the library, and the Internet. Fill in the information on the chart.

| School/Training Program | Classes | Length of Classes | Costs |
|---|---|---|---|
| | | | |
| | | | |
| | | | |
| | | | |
| | | | |
| | | | |
| | | | |

**B** Which schools and classes do you want to learn more about? Select one school and make a list of three or four questions you want to ask. Then write a letter requesting more information about the programs that are available.

(your address)
(your city, state, zip code)

(date)

(name of school)
(address of school)

To Whom It May Concern:

    I would like to get more information about your training classes in

_____. Could you send me information about

_____

_____

_____?

Sincerely yours,

_____

(your signature)

**C** When you receive information from the school, share it with your classmates.

**D** Work in groups of four. Focus on one person at a time.
1. Find out about each person's past work, present work, and future plans.
2. Find out what he or she is good at and what he or she needs to learn.
3. Then fill in the charts.

1.

| Name | Past Job Experience | Present Job | Future Plans |
|------|---------------------|-------------|--------------|
| Maria | secretary | housewife | bilingual secretary |
| | | | |
| | | | |
| | | | |
| | | | |

**2.**

| NAME | STRENGTHS | WEAKNESSES |
|---|---|---|
| Maria | can organize papers, can type, can answer phones | doesn't know computers yet |
|  |  |  |
|  |  |  |
|  |  |  |

**E** Discuss the information gathered about each person in 5D. If you were a job counselor, what education and training would you suggest for each team member? Explain.

| NAME | IDEAS FOR EDUCATION AND TRAINING | WHERE? | WHEN? |
|---|---|---|---|
|  |  |  |  |
|  |  |  |  |
|  |  |  |  |

# 6. Listening at Work

**A** A supervisor is giving information about training classes to his employees. Listen to the information and fill in the schedule.

| CLASS | BEGINNING DATE | BEGINNING TIME | LOCATION |
|---|---|---|---|
| **1.** Math and Reading (1st shift) | September 19th |  |  |
| **2.** Math and Reading (2nd shift) |  | 9:00 P.M. |  |
| **3.** English as a Second Language |  |  | at the factory |
| **4.** Air Conditioning and Heating Repair |  |  | Main Street School |
| **5.** Machine Shop |  | 1:00 P.M. |  |
| **6.** High School Diploma and GED Preparation |  | 3:00 P.M. |  |
| **7.** Auto Body Repair |  |  | Sammy's Auto Repair |

**B** Listen to the tape again. Think of four questions to ask the supervisor about the factory closing. Practice the questions and answers with a partner. Act out the interview in front of the class.

# 7. Problem Solving

**A** Review the main points in Jesus's story (2B). Talk about these questions with your classmates. Write your answers.

In 1986 conditions on Jesus's job were bad. What were some of the problems?

1. _polluted factory air_

2. _____

3. _____

4. _____

**B** Computerized machines were installed in Jesus's factory in 1993. What are some benefits of computerized machines? What are some health problems workers can develop from working on computerized machines all day? Fill in the chart. Then discuss ideas on how to solve the problems.

| BENEFITS | HEALTH PROBLEMS |
|---|---|
| 1. machines do the work | eye problems |
| 2. | |
| 3. | |
| 4. | |

★ **C** Think about more work situations in which computerized machines are used. Are computerized machines more **harmful** or more **beneficial** to workers? Why? Write a paragraph giving three reasons in support of your opinion. Read your paragraph to your classmates.

**Definitions**

harmful  damaging

beneficial  helpful

**D** Work Culture Notes:

### The Changing Technology of the Workplace

Much work that used to be done by hand is now done by machines. In many companies, robots and computers have taken the place of humans. What can workers who are losing jobs do? Training on the job, **retraining** for a new job, and continually taking classes to learn new **skills** are ways workers can help themselves. The more skills a worker has, the more she or he will be in demand in the workforce.

**Definitions**

retraining  to reeducate in a new skill

skill  ability to do something, for example, fix a car

### Job Changes and New Careers

In the past, an individual would find a job and stay at that job all his or her life. Now, for many workers, changing jobs every few years is becoming a way of life. Some people change jobs within a company. Some workers change companies to get a better job. Some people leave jobs to return to school for training classes so they can get better jobs. Some people continue working and take training classes at the same time until they can move up to better jobs.

# 8. Understanding the Workplace

**A** Work with a partner. Read each statement. Decide if it is true or false or if you don't know. Put a checkmark in that column. You and your partner may have different answers.

| | TRUE | FALSE | DON'T KNOW |
|---|---|---|---|
| 1. If a company adds new machines, every worker is retrained for a new job. | | | |
| 2. When a company adds new technology, some jobs are eliminated. | | | |
| 3. More work opportunities will always be available if you continue to learn new skills. | | | |
| 4. In most corporations a worker can be **promoted** without additional training. | | | |
| 5. New machines always create new jobs. | | | |
| 6. All training classes cost money. | | | |
| 7. Everyone can learn to operate a computer. | | | |
| 8. Some people are better at working with their hands than with their minds. | | | |
| 9. There are many schools that have courses that train people to operate new machinery. | | | |

**Definition**

promoted
moved
from a
lower to
a higher
position

**B** Now discuss each answer with the class. Pick a different student to lead the discussion of each question.

**C** Employers want to know about the specific skills of each job applicant. Pick a specific job. Tell your partner about the job and the skills it requires. Practice asking and answering questions with a partner.

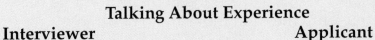

### Talking About Experience

| Interviewer | Applicant |
|---|---|
| 1. *Have you had* any experience operating an electric saw? | Yes, *I've had* many years of experience using an electric saw. I used one in my native country. |
| 2. *Have you ever used* a computer? | No, *I've never used* a computer. But I am a very quick learner. |

For more help with **talking about experience,** turn to the **Grammar Appendix.**

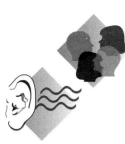

**D** Work in groups of four. Imagine you are career advisors. Listen to each speaker. Discuss what each speaker can do. Listen to each situation again. Choose one situation to act out.

Advances in technology may affect every job in the future. What should each worker do?

1. What should Margarita do?
   a. Look for a new job
   b. Take the training class and pay a babysitter
   c. Bring her children to the class with her
   d. Get information about programs that might help her change jobs

2. What can David do?
   a. Ask other workers on the job for help
   b. Ask the supervisor for additional help
   c. Stay on the job while getting more training at school
   d. Ask to observe another worker before or after his regular hours

3. What can Tatiana do?
   a. Say nothing and wait for more information
   b. Ask the supervisor if the rumors are true
   c. Ask other workers about the rumors
   d. Find out about job placement programs for older workers

4. What can Chen do?
   a. Look for another job and hope his English improves
   b. Study English as a Second Language at school
   c. Study English as a Second Language at home on television
   d. Ask his children to translate for him

★ **E** Write an example of a work problem. Submit it to another group for problem-solving advice.

# 9. Understanding Work Graphs

**A** In Chapter 2 you saw that the number of jobs in some occupations was increasing. In other occupations the number of jobs is decreasing. Read the information on the graph below.

### DECREASES IN EMPLOYMENT 1994-2005

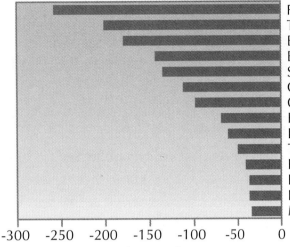

Farmers
Typists and word processors
Bookkeeping, accounting, and clerks
Bank tellers
Sewing machine operators
Cleaners and servants, private household
Computer operators
Billing, posting, and calculating machine operators
Duplicating, mail, and other office machine operators
Textile machine operators
File clerks
Freight, stock, and material movers
Farm workers
Machine tool cutting operators and tenders, metal and plastic

-300   -250   -200   -150   -100   -50   0

Thousands

**Definition**

downsizing
decrease
the number
of workers

Between 1994 and 2005, many workers will lose jobs because of technological advances and organizational **downsizing.** For example, the number of people doing word processing will decrease because there will be increases in both new office machines and the number of professionals who do their own work.

Source: *Occupational Outlook Handbook 1996–1997*, p. 4.

**B** Answer these questions using the information in the graph.

1. What does a decrease in employment mean? _____

_____

2. Which occupation will be losing the most employees?

_____

How many jobs will be lost? _____

3. List the top five occupations that will lose employees.

_____

4. What is causing typists and word processors to lose jobs?

_____

★ 5. Why do you think so many farmers are losing their jobs?

_____

★ 6. What do you think is causing most jobs to be lost?

_____

★ 7. Which jobs or companies have left your neighborhood? Why?

_____

_____

★ **C** With your teacher and classmates, write a letter to your local newspaper. Explain which jobs or companies have left your area. Give your opinion about why you think this is happening and what can be done about it. Use vocabulary from your vocabulary database.

## 10. Workplace Vocabulary

| | | |
|---|---|---|
| downsizing | computerized | technical |
| technological advances | decrease | physical |
| training | experience | robots |

**A** Fill in the following sentences using the workplace vocabulary. Compare your answers with your classmates. Then find the pages where the words are used and fill in the page numbers. Compare the sentences you found with the sentences on this page.

Page Number

1. Raul took a _____ class to learn to operate a forklift.   _____

2. The number of workers at the insurance company went from 1000 to 750. There was a _____ of 250 workers.   _____

3. Lifting and moving a lot of boxes is _____ labor.   _____

4. Raj made furniture in his country for 15 years. He has a lot of _____ working with wood.   _____

5. A company that is reducing its number of workers is _____.   _____

6. At a _____ school classes are available in nursing, electronics, and truck driving.   _____

7. In some factories _____ may do the work of humans.   _____

8. Many jobs used to be done by hand. Now they are _____.   _____

9. Because of _____ _____ many positions have been combined into one job.   _____

**B** Select two words from the vocabulary list. Write each word on a piece of paper. Ask another student to give a definition of a word and to use the word in a sentence. When you finish with one student, move to another and repeat.

# 11. Assessing Your Progress

**A** Answer the following questions.

1. What are three benefits of computerized machines?

   _____

   _____

2. What are three harmful effects of computerized machines?

   _____

   _____

3. What machines do you have experience using? For how long did you use them?

   _____

4. Name three things that workers can do to prepare for the technology of the future.

   _____

   _____

5. Name two places you can go for training for future jobs.

   _____    _____

6. Name four jobs you think will be good to have in the future.

   _____  _____  _____  _____

7. From what you learned about technology and training, what are your personal plans for your future job(s) and training?

   _____

   _____

# 12. Looking Back

| **A** Things I learned about technology and training | How I can apply what I learned to my life |
|---|---|
| 1. | |
| 2. | |
| 3. | |
| **B** New words and idioms | Related words from my job |
| 1. | |
| 2. | |
| 3. | |

# 4 COMMUNICATING WITH YOUR BOSS

## 1. Talking About Work

▲ **Look at the pictures. Discuss these questions with your teacher and class.**

> ▶ What is happening in the pictures?
> ▶ How do you think the worker feels?
> ▶ What do you think the chef will say to the owner?
> ★ ▶ What would you do if you were in this situation?

**A** Discuss the words with your teacher and classmates. Write your ideas on the lines.

} good boss    bad boss {

**B** Read

▲ Knarik Shahbazian

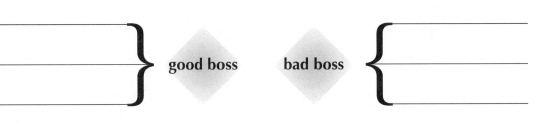

**Reading Strategy: Scan for Information**

Look at the story quickly and find the answers to these questions.

1. What is the title?
2. Who is the author?
3. Who is the story about?
4. Which three words describe the choir director?
5. Where did the choir travel?
6. How did audiences respond to the concerts?

## Definitions

**choir** a group of singers

**accuracy** precision

**rehearsal** practice session

**strict** expects rules to be followed

**petrified** very afraid

**praise** to tell someone they did a good job

**reward** something positive given for something done well

**perform** to give a public presentation

**My Singing Career** by Knarik Shahbazian

In Armenia I sang in a **choir**. I sang in that choir for 15 years, from the time I was 25 until I was 40.

Our maestro, Mr. Sedrak Kazarian, the "boss" of our choir, had a strong personality. He liked **accuracy**. We had **rehearsals** with him every day. My boss was **strict** about everybody learning his or her part of the music. He didn't like laziness. Sometimes he got angry. When he stood in front of the choir, everybody stopped talking because they were **petrified**.

In reality, the maestro was a kind and excellent man. When I asked him for help with my singing, he sang my part for me and showed me how to do it. When we made mistakes, he told us to practice more. When we sang extremely well, he **praised** us and said he felt proud. He didn't give praise very often.

The **reward** for our good work was to travel to the Ukraine and several Baltic cities to sing. Actually we **performed** on the stages of many different countries. Audiences greeted our concerts with great acclaim. Many articles were written about my boss. Different magazines praised him and his art as a great musician and conductor.

# 3. Thinking About the Story

**A** Talk about these questions with a partner.

1. What was Knarik's profession?
2. How does she describe her "boss" (paragraph 2)?
3. How did the other singers feel when the maestro was leading the choir?
4. What did the maestro do to help Knarik with her singing?
★ 5. How do you think the maestro communicated with the singers?

**B** Read Knarik's story again. With a partner, make a list of all the words she uses to describe her "boss." Then list words you would use to describe your boss or someone else's boss.

| KNARIK'S BOSS | A BOSS YOU KNOW | |
|---|---|---|
| | | |
| | | |
| | | |

Share your lists with your classmates. Add any new words to your list.

**C** Work in a group of four. Write each word from 3B on an index card. Categorize the cards into two groups, positive and negative. Discuss why you think each quality is positive or negative in a boss. Report your list to the class.

★ **D** With your group, decide which three qualities are the most important in a boss and why. Report your group's decisions to the class.

**E** Read Knarik's story again and review the vocabulary in 2B. Circle any new words. Add these words to the **work dictionary** in your notebook or to the vocabulary database in your computer. Write the meaning next to each word. Use it in a sentence.

| Word | Meaning | Sentence |
|---|---|---|
| *reward* | something positive given for something done well | His reward for working hard was praise from his supervisor. |

# 4. After the Story

**A** Survey the class with the following questions. Record the answers.

| Class Survey | Number of Students |
|---|---|
| **1.** How many students would prefer a boss who is strict and strong? | _____ |
| **2.** How many students would prefer a boss who is easygoing and nice? | _____ |
| **3.** How many students would prefer to be their own boss? | _____ |

**B** Talk about the following questions with your team. Write the answers.

**1.** Why do some workers prefer a boss who is strict and strong?

_____

**2.** Why do some workers prefer a boss who is easygoing and nice?

_____

**3.** What can you do if you have a mean boss or a boss you don't get along with?

_____

**4.** Why do some people prefer to be their own boss?

_____

**C** Review the survey in 4A. With your teacher and class, make a bar graph from the information.

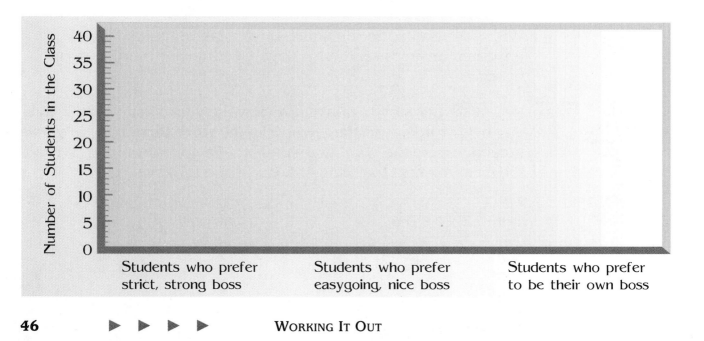

Number of Students in the Class

40
35
30
25
20
15
10
5
0

Students who prefer strict, strong boss · Students who prefer easygoing, nice boss · Students who prefer to be their own boss

**D** Change the numbers in 4C to percentages. Your teacher will help you.

1. What percentage of students want a boss who is strict and strong? _____
2. What percentage of students want a boss who is easygoing and nice? _____
3. What percentage of students would prefer to be their own boss? _____

# 5. Receiving, Repeating, and Checking Information

**A** **Work Culture Notes:**

**Communication Between Worker and Boss**

Good communication between a worker and a supervisor is essential on any job.

**Definitions**

**be efficient** do something without wasting time, energy, or money

**be flexible** able to change easily

1. Use polite English when you are talking.
2. Find out what your job responsibilities are. Know what you are supposed to do every day.
3. Make sure your instructions are clear. Make sure you understand what is said to you.
4. Find out the order in which you are expected to do the work.
5. **Be efficient.**
6. **Be flexible.** Do what you are asked to do.
7. Report work accidents to the boss.

**B** Practice asking a supervisor for clarification of work instructions.

*Asking for Clarification*

*Do you mean I must* check my machine first and then begin a new setup?
*Did you say to* remove all the fruit and vegetables that look old?
*Do you want me to* work on this letter first, or answer the phones?

For more help with **checking information**, turn to the **Grammar Appendix**.

**C** Below are examples of what an employer may ask an employee to do on the job. Student A is the employer giving instructions. (Look at the sentences below.) Student B is the employee, listening and repeating the information. (Student B do *not* look at the sentences.) Practice giving instructions and receiving information. Then switch roles.

**Example:**

Employer: Don't forget to park in the employee section between the green lines.

Worker: *Did you say to* park between the green lines in the employee section?

1. Please polish the floors in rooms 105, 107, and 109. After that, take a break.
2. Don't forget to count all the money in the cash register at the end of every day. Then list it on the register sheet.
3. Do a tune-up and an oil change on the car in stall number 2. Check the brakes too.
4. Please draw some blood from the patient in room 405 and bring the sample back to the laboratory for testing.
5. Return all five electric drills to the tool room and sign them in on the list.

**D** Listen to the conversations. Circle who you think is speaking.

1. **a.** contractor      **b.** painter
2. **a.** nurse      **b.** nursing assistant
3. **a.** supervisor      **b.** newspaper delivery person
4. **a.** housekeeper      **b.** homemaker
5. **a.** store manager      **b.** supermarket stocker

Listen to the conversations again. What was each person asked to do?

1. **a.** paint the bathroom      **b.** paint the living room
2. **a.** contact a doctor      **b.** call the police
3. **a.** quit      **b.** continue to do the same good work
4. **a.** buy window cleaner      **b.** buy paper towels
5. **a.** continue to do the same good work      **b.** be flexible

# 6. Inventory: Reporting Problems

**A** Look at this list of work problems. Which of these problems would you talk to your supervisor about? Discuss your answers in teams of three.

| | REPORT | DON'T REPORT | NOT SURE |
|---|---|---|---|
| **1.** Chemicals spilled on the floor | | | |
| **2.** Your machine is broken | | | |
| **3.** A coworker isn't doing his or her job and you have to do extra work | | | |
| **4.** You don't understand some instructions from the supervisor | | | |
| **5.** Your mother is very sick in the hospital and you need to leave work | | | |

**B** In your team, give examples of four additional problems you may want to talk about with a supervisor.

_____

_____

_____

_____

**C** Now give examples of four problems you could solve without talking to a supervisor.

_____

_____

_____

_____

★ **D** Work in a group. Review 6A, 6B, and 6C. Think about a problem that you would or would not take to a boss in your home country. Explain both the problem and your reasons to your group. Each person has two minutes to talk.

# 7. Working on Mistakes

▲ Sushi

## Definitions

**sushi** raw fish and rice, popular in Japan

**bankrupt** to have to close a business because you are unable to pay the bills

**fired** to be terminated from a job

**sake** Japanese liquor made from rice

**receipt** paper showing a bill is paid

**apologize** to say you are sorry for something you did

**A** Read the story.

### Learning to Understand My Boss by Kazou Imai

My boss is a **sushi** chef and also the owner of a small restaurant. He was very strict when I started to work there as a waiter and cashier. If I made a mistake, he got upset. One time, after I gave a customer too much change, he told me, "If you do this again, my sushi bar will be **bankrupt**!" I didn't say anything back to him. I thought if I said anything, I would be **fired**.

Now I have been working here for a while. Last week a regular customer came in and ordered sushi, sake, and egg custard for dessert. That man orders the same thing every time he comes in. After the customer left, my boss said I forgot to charge the man for the **sake** and the egg custard. He showed me the **receipt** from a different customer. He was upset. I was upset, too. I looked and looked for the correct receipt. Later I found it and showed it to my boss. My boss said, "I'm sorry."

In general, my boss seems very happy making sushi. He goes to the restaurant even on his days off to prepare food for the next day. A lot of the same customers come back to his restaurant to eat his sushi. He talks to the customers and makes them laugh. Now when there are no customers in the restaurant, my boss and I sit on the stools in front of the sushi bar. He tells me stories about his life and about life in Japan. He's a nice boss.

**B** Discuss these questions in a group. Write down your answers.

1. What mistake did Kazou make when he started his job?

_____

2. What did the boss say when Kazou made a mistake?

_____

3. What did Kazou do?

_____

4. What other mistake did the boss think Kazou made?

_____

5. What did Kazou do?

_____

★ 6. How did the boss **apologize** for his mistake?

_____

**C** In your group, talk about mistakes that are made at work. What are the mistakes? What does the boss say? How do workers respond to the boss?

Do you know of any situations in which a boss blamed a worker for things the worker didn't do? Talk about what happened.

**D** Your teacher will ask some students to discuss mistakes they see at work. Give suggestions on how to correct the mistakes.

| MISTAKE | SUGGESTIONS |
| --- | --- |
| *errors in work* | *team members check their work before it leaves work area* |
|  |  |
|  |  |
|  |  |

 **E** Make a note on your calendar that in one month the same students will report back to the class about the mistakes they observed and what has happened.

## 8. Situations

 **A** Below are some positive and negative comments your supervisor might make about your work. Draw a line to the appropriate response. Check your answers with a partner.

1. We're very pleased with your work performance. I'm going to recommend you for a pay increase.

2. The rule is, "No eating on the job." The next time I catch you eating, I'll have to write you up.

3. I've noticed your production is down. Are you having a problem with your machine?

4. The last customer told me you were an excellent salesperson.

a. Sorry. I didn't know that rule.

b. Thanks.

c. Thanks for telling me that. That's a real compliment.

d. The machine broke down yesterday afternoon. It was just fixed this morning.

**B** The following are situations in which it is necessary for a boss and a worker to communicate. Sit in a small group. Read and act out the scenes. After each scene, talk about what happened between the worker and the boss.

1. Ramona has worked as a housekeeper at the Stadium Hotel for four years. She receives many compliments from hotel guests for her good work. Her annual evaluations are always excellent. She would like a promotion to a supervisory position. The company has a history of filling top positions with men.
   What does Ramona say to her supervisor, John?
   What does he tell her?

2. Vesna is a secretary in a medical office. Her work is organized and accurate. Unfortunately, her boss thinks she is not a good worker. He says her work is never finished on time. She hears from a coworker that he wants to hire someone to replace her.
   What does Vesna say to her supervisor?
   How does the boss respond?

3. Shiro is the most experienced mechanic at Wong's Auto Shop. Recently he has been absent a lot from work. For the past three days he has been out and hasn't called. Last month he was absent 4 of 20 work days. His supervisor, Sammy, talks to him about the problem.
   What does the supervisor say?
   What reason does Shiro give for his absences?
   What is the supervisor's response?

4. Jesse is the supervisor at the airport restaurant. All food must be well prepared and sanitary. Most food workers wear the required hair nets and aprons, but Jesse notices a few workers are not.
   What should she tell the workers?
   What do they say to her?

5. Charlie has worked with a construction crew building houses for six years. Lately he has been working very slowly and smoking and drinking on the job. His slow work and dangerous habits make it impossible for the crew to complete the work on time.
   What does the supervisor, Ralph, say to Charlie?
   How does Charlie respond?

6. John is a waiter at a hotel restaurant. His boss has said no one can take a break during a four-hour shift. Sometimes John would like to sit down, go to the bathroom, or call his family, but he is not allowed to do that. Lately his legs have been hurting a lot. He knows the labor law requires his boss to give him a break every two hours.
   What does he say to the supervisor?
   How does the supervisor respond?

# 9. Work Memos

**A** Work with a partner. Read the memo.

## Definitions

**hiring freeze** to stop employing new workers

**cost reduction** to decrease the money spent

**skyrocketing** increasing very quickly

**funds** money

**vacant** empty

**staff** all the workers at a workplace

---

**TYLER COUNTY** Hospital

### INTER-OFFICE MEMORANDUM

TO:      All Clinic, Hospital, and Nursing Staff
FROM: Art Torres, Personnel Director
RE:      **Hiring Freeze** and **Cost Reduction**
DATE:   Feb 1, 1998

Recently, the costs of buying new medical equipment for our hospital have been **skyrocketing**. The equipment costs have exhausted our **funds**.

Because of the increasing costs, we cannot fill any **vacant** jobs at this time. There will be a temporary **hiring freeze** in all departments. We hope to add more **staff** in the near future.

We are looking for suggestions from you, our staff, for how to reduce costs in every department. Please submit your written suggestions for **cost reduction** to your departmental supervisor. The department that reduces costs the most over the next three months will receive an award.

---

**B** Answer these questions about the memo.

1. What is the problem with medical equipment costs?

   _____

   _____

2. How will a hiring freeze affect the employees?

   _____

   _____

3. What would you suggest to reduce hospital costs?

   _____

   _____

★ 4. What additional information would you need to make more suggestions?

   _____

   _____

★ 5. What could the employees say to Art Torres?

   _____

   _____

# 10. What We Say at Work

**A** Listen to the conversation. Put a check (✔) next to the items you hear about in the talk.

|  | ITEM MENTIONED | WHO TO CONTACT |
|---|---|---|
| stapler |  |  |
| paper and pencils |  |  |
| calendar |  |  |
| computer |  |  |
| business cards |  |  |
| fax machine |  |  |
| tape |  |  |
| copier |  |  |
| name tags |  |  |
| time records |  |  |
| coffee club |  |  |
| party |  |  |
| restrooms |  |  |
| lunch |  |  |
| telephone calls |  |  |

**B** Listen to the conversation again and write the names of the people or departments you are supposed to contact. Use **S** for supervisor, **R** for repair department, and **P** for the party organizer.

# 11. Workplace Vocabulary

| apologize | efficient | praises |
|-----------|-----------|---------|
| mistake | strict | freeze |
| repeat | communicate | fired |

**A** Fill in the following sentences using the workplace vocabulary. Compare your answers with your classmates. Then find the pages where the words are used and write in the page numbers. Compare the sentences you found with the sentences on this page.

**Page Number**

1. A worker should _____ frequently with a boss. _____

2. If you destroy something you are working on, you have made a _____. _____

3. When you do your work well without wasting time, you are very _____. _____

4. If a supervisor asks an employee to say the same thing again, the boss is asking the worker to _____ the information. _____

5. If you lose your job because you do bad work, you have been _____. _____

6. When you make a mistake on the job, the best thing to do is _____. _____

7. A person who wants everything done exactly right is very _____. _____

8. A company has jobs available but stops hiring. They are having a hiring _____. _____

9. A supervisor _____ an employee when she says, "You have done good work." _____

**B** Select two words from the list. Write each word on a piece of paper. Ask one student to give a definition of one word and to use the word in a sentence. Then ask another student to define the second word and use it in a sentence.

*Example:*  *Question:* What does **communicate** mean?
*Answer:* It means to talk with another person.
*Question:* Please use **communicate** in a sentence.
*Answer:* The worker **communicates** a safety problem to the boss.

# 12. Assessing Your Progress

**A** Answer the following questions.

1. List six characteristics of a good boss.

   _____  _____  _____

   _____  _____  _____

2. Write two questions asking for clarification of a supervisor's instructions.

   _____

   _____

3. What are three possible communication problems you may have with a boss?

   _____  _____  _____

4. Give an example of a mistake you made on the job or at home. What did you do? What did your supervisor or family members do?

   _____

   _____

5. What is something positive a supervisor can say about an employee's work?

   _____

6. What is something negative a supervisor can say about an employee's work?

   _____

# 13. Looking Back

| **A** Things I learned about communicating with my boss | How I can apply what I learned to my life |
|---|---|
| 1. | |
| 2. | |
| 3. | |
| **B** New words and idioms | Related words from my job |
| 1. | |
| 2. | |
| 3. | |

# 5 WORK IN MY HOME COUNTRY, WORK IN MY NEW COUNTRY

## 1. Talking About Work

▲ **Look at the pictures. Discuss these questions with your teacher and class.**

> ▶ What two jobs do you see in the pictures?
> ▶ What are the differences between the two jobs?
> ▶ Which job do you think gives the worker more satisfaction?
> ★ ▶ Why do some people take a different kind of job when they move to another country?
> ★ ▶ Do you think it is easy or difficult to adapt to a different job in a new country? Why?

# 2. Work Stories

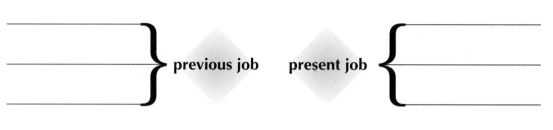

**A** Discuss the words with your teacher and classmates. Write your ideas on the lines.

_____  
_____ } previous job ◆ present job { _____  
_____

**B** Read

▲ Giovanni Castro

## Definition

**skilled** to be good at doing something

**Reading Strategy: Scan for Information**

Read the story quickly.
Find the answers to these questions.

1. What was Giovanni's job in Mexico?
2. What is his job in the United States?
3. What does he want to do in the future?

### My Work as a Carpenter in Mexico
by Giovanni Castro

I was a carpenter in my hometown in Mexico. I learned the job from my friend, Cesar. He was a good carpenter with a lot of experience.

I was interested in learning to work with my hands and I wanted to learn all about wood. I liked my job because I learned to make many different kinds of furniture. I always tried to do the best job that I could.

If you want to be a **skilled** carpenter, you need to know about all the tools. You need to know how to cut the wood and how to make it look beautiful. If you learn to be a good carpenter, people will respect your work.

## Working in the United States

After I came to the United States I worked in a factory making **blinds**. I learned to cut plastic and aluminum on an electric saw to make the blinds. When the factory had a lot of orders, I went to the customers' homes and **installed** the blinds. I worked very hard. I learned how to work in a factory and how to work with customers.

From each job, here and in Mexico, I've learned new skills. I've learned to be responsible for my own work and to be independent. Saving money has been a **priority**. I want to start my own company making blinds. That is my plan for the future.

### Definitions

**blind** covering for a window made of strips of plastic or aluminum

**install** to put something in place

**priority** the most important thing to do

## 3. Thinking About the Story

**A** Talk about these questions in a group.

1. Compare Giovanni's job as a carpenter with his job making blinds. What is the same and what is different about the two jobs?

2. What size company do you think he will own in five years? Why?

**B** Giovanni tells us that saving money is his priority. Talk about the following questions in your group. Then use your ideas from the discussion to help you write a paragraph about Giovanni.

Why is it necessary for him to save money now?
How will he save money?
How much money do you think he needs to start his own company?
What are some of the things he will have to pay for when he starts his own company?

**C** Read the story again. Circle any new words. Add these words to the **work dictionary** in your notebook or to the vocabulary database in your computer. Write the meaning next to each word. Use it in a sentence.

| Word | Meaning | Sentence |
|------|---------|----------|
| *skilled* | to be good at doing something | The carpenter was skilled at making tables. |

# 4. After the Story

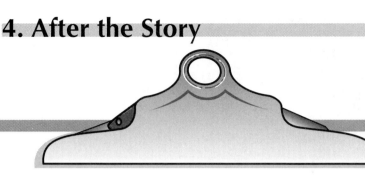

**A** **Work Culture Notes: Changing Jobs—Starting a New Career**

Workers in the United States will look for jobs, or "job hunt," approximately eight times in their lives. Many want to start new careers.

To look for a job or find a new career you need to take a **personal inventory**. Evaluate your skills, your past work history, and your job preferences. Then use what you have discovered about yourself to help you in your job search.

> **Definition**
>
> **personal inventory**
> a list of
> personal skills
> and job
> preferences

1. Skills
   * Are you good at working with people, information, or machines?
   * What specific machines do you know how to use?
   * Do you like to work with other people or alone?
   * What is your level of English?

2. Job history and experience
   * What jobs or work experience have you had before?
   * What kinds of companies have you worked for? (What industries have you worked in?)

3. Preferences
   * What shift do you want to work?
   * Where would you like to work? (office, school, hospital, restaurant, store, hotel, factory, construction)
   * What salary do you need to earn?

**B** Think about your work experience or another person's experience. Your teacher will read the questions. Write your answers. Then ask a partner the questions. Listen and write his or her answers.

| | You | Your Partner |
|---|---|---|
| **1.** What job did you have in your home country? | | |
| **2.** What did you do on your job? | | |
| **3.** Did you like your job? | | |
| **4.** What is your job now? | | |
| **5.** What do you do on your job? | | |
| **6.** Do you like your present job? | | |
| **7.** List some skills that you have (see Work Culture Note 4A). | | |
| **8.** What job would you like to have in the future? | | |

**C** With your teacher and class do the following:

1. Make a list of all the jobs held by students in your class.

2. Form groups of students who have similar jobs. In the groups, discuss these questions:

   **a.** In what ways are the jobs in the United States like the jobs in your country?

   In what ways are the jobs in the United States different from the jobs in your country?

   **b.** What jobs would each of you like to have in five years?

   What can you do now to prepare for that job?

   ★ **c.** How can you work together with your classmates so all of you can find better jobs in the future?

**D** Fill in the timelines. On timeline 1, list your work experience. On timeline 2, list how you can prepare to get a better job. Include English classes, job training classes, earning money, and other plans.

**1.**

| **ten** years ago | **five** years ago | **two** years ago | **now** |
|---|---|---|---|

**2.** *study and learn English*

| **now** | **six** months from now | **one** year from now | **two** years from now | **five** years from now |
|---|---|---|---|---|

# 5. Skills Inventory

**A** Look over Giovanni's story again. When Giovanni was a carpenter in Mexico he made furniture. He **measured** and sawed the wood. He **drilled** holes and **pounded** nails into the wood. Then he **sanded** the wood.

With a partner, list what he does on his present job.

1. *He measures the windows.* _____

2. _____

3. _____

4. _____

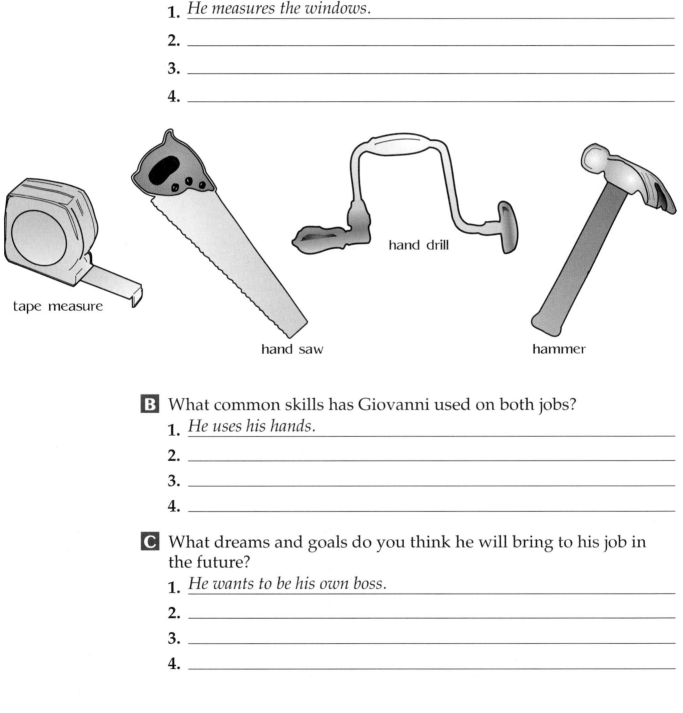

tape measure

hand saw

hand drill

hammer

**B** What common skills has Giovanni used on both jobs?

1. *He uses his hands.* _____

2. _____

3. _____

4. _____

**C** What dreams and goals do you think he will bring to his job in the future?

1. *He wants to be his own boss.* _____

2. _____

3. _____

4. _____

# 6. Choices

**A** Read the story.

▲ Manolo Saagastume

## Definitions

**crops** vegetables, fruits, or grains (foods that are grown for people or animals)

**cuff** a fold or band at the bottom of a sleeve

**Changing Careers** by Manolo Saagastume

In 1975 I worked as an administrative assistant for the Guatemalan Federation of Cooperatives. The Federation helped small farmers buy fertilizer to protect their **crops** from insects, to sell their crops for a good price, and to educate their children. On my job I did everything from cleaning offices to arranging educational meetings for the farmers. I also did some bookkeeping. In 1977 I was promoted from administrative assistant to assistant manager. I did all the hiring and firing of people in the organization and also kept track of finances.

In 1981, there was conflict between the military and other groups in my country. Some of the people working in our organization were killed. My brother-in-law invited me to come to the United States. I decided to leave Guatemala.

When I arrived here in 1982, my biggest problem was the language barrier. The only English I knew was "How are you?" The first job I got was for low pay. It was as a sewing machine operator. I made 2 cents for each **cuff** I sewed on a sleeve, $80.00 per week. By this time my wife and I had three children. It was difficult for us to make ends meet. I decided to go to school to learn English.

At night I studied ESL. Later, I passed the GED and got my high school diploma. I decided to go to college to study computers. I knew it would take a long time.

In 1986, while I was in still in college, one of my friends talked to me about selling real estate. I liked the idea because I already had experience working with people. With a high school diploma I could take real estate training classes, take the licensing exam, and have a real estate license in six months.

Now I have been a successful real estate agent since 1987. I help people find new homes. I help them understand the finances and what is involved in purchasing a new home.

My advice to you is this: if you want to get a good job, the first thing you have to do is learn English. You have to be able to speak the language. Second, grab the opportunities when they come. If you take the opportunities, you will move faster toward finding the right career. Finally, build on what you already know. I learned how to work with farmers in Guatemala. I learned how to manage money. When I decided to go into real estate, I used both of those things to my advantage.

**B** Look at Manolo's story again. Fill in the timeline. List the jobs Manolo had in Guatemala and the jobs he has had in the United States. List his years in school.

| | | | | |
|---|---|---|---|---|
| 1975 | 1977 | 1982 | 1987 | now |

**C** List the skills Manolo developed to help him in his new career in the United States.

1. *learning how to work with people* _____

2. _____

3. _____

4. _____

5. _____

**D** What are some reasons why Manolo started a career in real estate after he came to the United States? Talk about this question and write down your answer.

_____

_____

_____

_____

_____

**E** Work in a group. Compare Manolo's work in the cooperative in Guatemala to his work as a real estate agent in the United States. Discuss these questions.

1. How many hours a day do you think he worked in the cooperative? with home buyers?

2. What problems do you think he had in working with farmers? with home buyers?

3. What language did he use on-the-job in Guatemala? on-the-job in the United States?

4. Do you think he felt satisfied at the end of his work day in Guatemala? in the United States?

# 7. Career and Changes

**A** Talk about the questions in your group: Did you or someone you know change to a new career after coming to the United States? Why did you or the other person make a change to a new job? Each person has two minutes to talk. After each person has spoken, write your answer.

**B** Your teacher will ask some students to discuss their career histories, their jobs in their native countries, and their jobs in the United States with the class. On the chalkboard and in your notebook, fill in the information about your classmates.

| NAME | JOB IN NATIVE COUNTRY | JOB IN UNITED STATES | FUTURE PLANS |
|------|----------------------|---------------------|--------------|
|      |                      |                     |              |
|      |                      |                     |              |
|      |                      |                     |              |

**C** Listen to each worker's story. Listen for the reason why each moved from one country to another. Circle the correct answers.

1. **a.** religious reasons      **b.** political reasons
2. **a.** war      **b.** family reasons
3. **a.** religious reasons      **b.** economic reasons
4. **a.** religious reasons      **b.** war

# 8. Real-life Situations

**A** Describe yourself by filling in the blanks below.

My name is _____. I am from _____.
In my native country I was a _____. I could _____
_____ on that job. I had that job for _____ years. I
_____ that job because _____.
  (liked/didn't like)

I was _____ years old when I came to the United States. I left my native country because _____.

*(continued on next page)*

In this country I have experience as a _____. I can
                                              (job)
_____. I have done this work for _____ years/months.
I _____ this job because _____.
    (like/don't like)
After my English is better, I would like to work as a _____.
I am doing _____ now so I can have a
better job in the future.

**B** The following questions are frequently asked in job interviews. Practice the questions with a partner. Practice describing yourself, using the information from 8A.

*Talking About the Past*

| **Interviewer:** | **Applicant:** |
| --- | --- |
| 1. Where *did* you *work* before? | I *worked* at Jim's Auto Repair. |
| 2. What *did* you *do* on that job? | |
| 3. What *did* you *like* most about the job? | |
| 4. Who *was* your boss? | |
| 5. How long *were* you there? | |
| 6. Why *did* you *leave* that job? | |
| ★ 7. Why *do* you *want* this job? | |
| ★ 8. What work would you like to be doing in five years? | |

For more help with **talking about the past**, turn to the **Grammar Appendix**.

# 9. What We Say at Work

**A** Work with a partner. Read the reasons for leaving a job. Decide if each reason is appropriate or inappropriate to tell a job interviewer. Make a check (✔) under appropriate or inappropriate. Talk about your answers with your class.

| | APPROPRIATE REASON | INAPPROPRIATE REASON |
|---|---|---|
| 1. I found a better job with higher pay. | | |
| 2. I wanted a job with more responsibility. | | |
| 3. I didn't get along with my coworkers. | | |
| 4. I left because I hurt my back. | | |
| 5. I was pregnant. | | |
| 6. I was laid off. | | |
| 7. I was fired because I was late too many times. | | |
| 8. My boss didn't like me. | | |
| 9. I came to the United States. | | |
| 10. I wanted a job with more independence. | | |

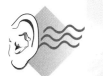

**B** Listen to these job interviews. What does each worker say about his or her reason for leaving the last job? Circle the appropriate answer.

1. **a.** She moved to a new country.  **b.** She was laid off.

2. **a.** He was fired.  **b.** He had a work accident.

3. **a.** Because she had a work accident.  **b.** Because she wanted a better job.

4. **a.** Because she had family problems.  **b.** Because she didn't like the job.

5. **a.** He was fired.  **b.** He was laid off.

6. **a.** Because she had a personal injury.  **b.** Because she had family problems.

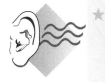

★ **C** Listen to each job interview again with a partner. Continue each dialogue between interviewer and job applicant. The interviewer asks about experience and education. The applicant answers. Act out the interview in front of your class.

# 10. Working with Application Forms

**A** If Manolo looks for another job, he will have to fill out an application form.

| Name | Job | Duties | Dates | Why Left |
|---|---|---|---|---|
| Manolo Saagastume | **1.** administrative assistant and assistant manager of cooperative | bookkeeping<br><br>hire and fire employees | 1975–81 | moved to U.S. |
| | **2.** real estate agent | sell property | 1986–present | ——— |

**B** Imagine you want to change jobs. Fill out the application form. List your current job and your last two jobs.

| Name | Job | Duties | Dates | Why Left |
|---|---|---|---|---|
| _____ | **1.** | | | |
| | | | | |
| | **2.** | | | |
| | | | | |

# 11. Understanding Charts: Immigration to the United States 1971–1990

**A** Work with the class. Read the information in the chart.

| IMMIGRATION FROM: | 1971–1980 | 1981–1990 |
|---|---|---|
| **1.** Europe and former Soviet Union | 801,300 | 705,600 |
| **2.** Asia and Middle East | 1,633,800 | 2,814,400 |
| **3.** North America and Central America | 1,645,000 | 3,125,000 |
| **4.** South America | 284,400 | 455,900 |
| **5.** Africa | 91,500 | 192,300 |

Source: *Statistical Abstract of the United States 1996,* p. 11.

**B** Answer these questions about the chart.

1. What years does the chart cover?

_____

2. Which section of the world had the largest immigration to the United States between 1971 and 1980? between 1981 and 1990?

_____

3. Which section of the world had the smallest immigration between 1971 and 1980? between 1981 and 1990?

_____

★ 4. Why do you think North America and Central America had the greatest increase in population coming to the United States?

_____

_____

★ 5. Did any area show a decrease in the number of immigrants coming to the United States between 1971 and 1990? Why do you think this happened?

_____

_____

## 12. Figure It Out

**A** Discuss the following problem in your team. Jose moved to the United States with his wife and child. He wants to give them a better life. What does Jose need to do now (within three months)? What does he need to do later (within two to five years)? Discuss your reasons. Compare your group's answers with those of other groups.

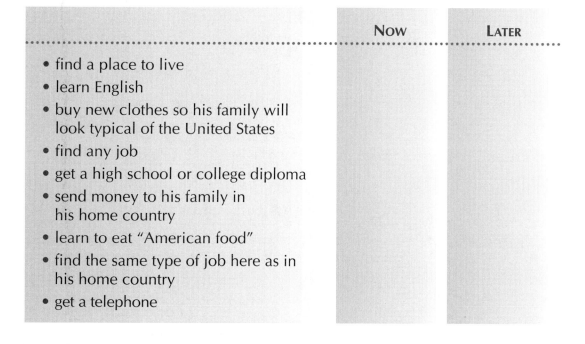

| | Now | Later |
|---|---|---|
| • find a place to live | | |
| • learn English | | |
| • buy new clothes so his family will look typical of the United States | | |
| • find any job | | |
| • get a high school or college diploma | | |
| • send money to his family in his home country | | |
| • learn to eat "American food" | | |
| • find the same type of job here as in his home country | | |
| • get a telephone | | |

## 13. Assessing Your Progress

**A** Answer the following questions.

1. Name the three parts of a personal inventory.

_____  _____  _____

2. Name three skills you used on a job in your country.

_____  _____  _____

3. Name three skills you use on your present job.

_____  _____  _____

4. Name two skills you would develop now to get a better job in the future.

_____  _____

5. What is an appropriate answer to the interview question, "Why did you leave your country?"

_____

6. Give two reasons why immigrants sometimes take different jobs when they go to a new country.

_____  _____

7. What are two appropriate reasons to give for leaving a job?

_____  _____

8. What are two inappropriate reasons to give for leaving a job?

_____  _____

## 14. Looking Back

| **A** Things I learned about my old job and my new job | How I can apply what I learned to my life |
| --- | --- |
| 1. | |
| 2. | |
| 3. | |
| **B** New words and idioms | Related words from my job |
| 1. | |
| 2. | |
| 3. | |

# 6 WORK SCHEDULES AND PAYCHECKS

## 1. Talking About Schedules

▲ **Look at the picture. Discuss these questions with your teacher and class.**

▶ What is the man thinking about?
▶ Is this man having an easy day?
★ ▶ Do you think this is a typical day in the United States?
★ ▶ Would his life be easier or more difficult if he lived in your country? Why?
▶ What are some things you have to do today?

# 2. Work Stories

**A** Discuss the words with your teacher and classmates. Write your ideas on the lines.

} work schedule    paycheck {

**B** Read

▲ Hoang Nguyen

## Definitions

**weld** to join metal pieces by melting

**time sheet** record of hours an employee has worked

**measurement** the size of something

### Reading Strategy: Ask Questions

1. Look at the picture.
2. Read the story title and the author's name.
3. Look at the key words.
4. Before you read the story, write four questions about the story and the author.

**My Work Schedule** by Hoang Nguyen

I worked as a clerk in the **welding** shop at my school, Rancho Santiago Community College, in Santa Ana, California. I went to school every day until 5:00 P.M. I started work after school and worked Monday to Thursday from 5:00 P.M. to 9:00 P.M. When I started at 5:00 P.M. I signed in on a **time sheet** and before I went home I signed out. I wrote the time on a time sheet. Next to the time I signed my initials.

Every day I did the same thing. First, I changed into my work clothes. Then I swept the work area and put equipment away in the closets. After that, the teachers gave me my work assignments. I cut materials for the welding students. The teachers gave me the exact **measurements** for the materials. I cut steel, aluminum, and other metals. I was lucky to have two very friendly bosses. They showed me how to operate the machines.

Every night I had a break from 7:00 P.M. to 7:15 P.M. My pay was $4.50 per hour. In 1991 that was higher than the minimum wage! My bosses never asked me to work overtime. I had vacations in the winter and in the summer.

I was paid every two weeks. I was so glad to hold the check in my hands! It was the first time in my life that I worked and earned money. I didn't have to ask my family to give me any money. When I got my paychecks, I bought things I couldn't afford before. I also sent money to my brother and sister and to my best friend in Vietnam. I worked at that job for about one year. Later, I moved to Minnesota.

## 3. Thinking About the Story

**A** Read the story again. Review the questions you wrote before the story. Can you answer your questions? If not, write new questions about the story.

_____

_____

_____

**B** Work in a group of four. Ask your classmates your original or revised questions. Listen and then answer their questions about the story.

★ **C** Investigate the following questions with your group: What are the laws in this state about paid breaks? about meal hours with pay? about days off? about overtime work with pay? Ask your teacher where to get more information. Summarize the information in the sentences below.

---

**BREAKS**

A worker gets a _____ minute break after working _____ hours.

It is _____.
  (paid/unpaid)

**MEAL HOUR**

A worker gets a meal hour after working _____ hours. It is _____.
  (paid/unpaid)

**EIGHT-HOUR DAY**

In an eight-hour day, a worker gets _____ breaks of _____ minutes each and _____ minutes for lunch.

**OVERTIME PAY**

After working _____ hours a week, a worker gets overtime pay.

---

**D** Read the story again. Circle any new words. Add these words to the **work dictionary** in your notebook or to the vocabulary database in your computer. Write the meaning next to each word. Use it in a sentence.

| Word | Meaning | Sentence |
|------|---------|----------|
| *time sheet* | record of hours an employee has worked | She signed her initials on the time sheet. |

## 4. Survey

**A** Discuss your work or daily schedule with members of your team.

1. Which days do you work?
2. How many hours do you work each day?
3. What time do you take a break? How long are your breaks? Are you paid during your breaks?
4. What time do you eat meals? How long do you take? Is your meal time paid?
5. Do you sign in and out on your job? Do you punch in and out at a time clock?
6. How many hours of overtime do you work? What is the pay for overtime?

**B** Complete the chart with information from your team. Use the questions above. Compare your answers with the answers of your classmates.

| | NAME | NAME | NAME | NAME |
|---|---|---|---|---|
| **DAYS OF WORK** | | | | |
| **HOURS OF WORK** | | | | |
| **BREAK TIME** | | | | |
| **MEAL TIME** | | | | |
| **OVERTIME** | | | | |

**C** Summarize the information in your team's chart. Do you and your classmates work the same number of hours? Do you work the same amount of overtime? Write sentences using your group's information.

**Summarizing Information**

*One of the* women in our group does housework. She doesn't punch a time clock.

*Four of the* students in our group work full time.

*None of the* people in our group works overtime.

*All of the* students in our group have breaks with pay.

For more help with **summarizing information,** turn to the **Grammar Appendix.**

★ **D** In 4A and 4B you talked about your present schedule. Now write five questions to find out what schedule another student would prefer to have.

**Examples:**

1. *Would you prefer to* work full time or part time? Why?
2. *What days would you prefer to* work?

★ **E** Interview other students. Find out their preferences. Write sentences about your classmates. Report the information back to your class.

**Example:**

Ali would prefer to work in the afternoon because _____

_____.

## 5. Personal Inventory—Schedule Changes and Days Off

**A** What are some acceptable reasons for requesting a day off or a change of work schedule? What are some unacceptable reasons? Read the situations below and add two more. Make a check (✔) under acceptable reason or unacceptable reason. Talk about your answers with a partner.

| | ACCEPTABLE REASON | UNACCEPTABLE REASON |
|---|---|---|
| **1.** Bing needs an afternoon off to go to a doctor's appointment. | | |
| **2.** Chen's best friend died. Chen wants to go to the funeral. | | |
| **3.** Lahn wants to change from the day shift to the night shift so she can take cosmetology classes in the daytime. | | |
| **4.** Igor's favorite soccer team is playing in an important championship. He wants to watch the game. | | |
| **5.** Ingrid wants to go to the bank every Friday morning to deposit her check. | | |
| **6.** Jenna wants to come 30 minutes later every day so she can walk her children to school. | | |
| **7.** | | |
| **8.** | | |

**B** Work in a group. Make sure at least one student in the group has experience with a change of work schedule.

1. Discuss this: When the student asked for a day off or for a change of work schedule, what happened? Include information about why the person needed the day off, what he or she said, what his or her supervisor said, and what happened.

2. Each group member will write the story as he or she hears it. Then each will read and compare stories to see if the information is correct.

When everyone is finished reading, group members will discuss when it is appropriate to ask for a change of schedule.

## 6. Situations—Company Policies and Schedules

**A** Sit in a small group. Listen to and read the scenes below. What should each worker do?

1. You are an *emergency room orderly* at County Hospital working the day shift. The orderly on the next shift calls in sick with the flu. Your supervisor asks you to work a second shift. You would receive time-and-a-half pay for every extra hour you work. Your problem is you are supposed to take your children to see their favorite Uncle Joe, who is visiting from out of town. Uncle Joe only comes to visit once every two years. He's 78 and you don't know when you will see him again.

   What should you do? Should you work overtime? Explain.

2. You are a *father with three children* and a lot of bills. You work the day shift at a car wash six days a week. Last week you worked as

a night security guard to make extra money. Every day for the last week you got to work late because you overslept. Your boss has told you that the next time you come to work late, you'll be fired.

What should you do? Should you continue to work the two jobs? Why?

3. Rosa is a *postal carrier* with three school-aged children. She has an urgent appointment to speak with her childrens' teachers at 6 P.M. At 4 P.M. she finishes delivering the mail. Her supervisor asks her if she can work an extra three hours and deliver the mail on another carrier's route.

What should Rosa do? Should she see her childrens' teachers or work the overtime?

4. Bob *teaches English as a Second Language* to adults. He works every morning, Monday to Friday, from 8:30 A.M. to 12:30 P.M. His wife is sick with cancer. When he comes to work he has trouble concentrating and frequently yells at his students. His supervisor meets with Bob and explains that Bob can't bring his personal problems to work.

What should Bob do? How can he concentrate on his work?

**B** Write a summary of your own situation. Describe a problem you have had and what you think you should do. After you finish writing, follow this procedure:

1. Ask a classmate to check your story and make suggestions for punctuation and correct verbs.

2. Make the necessary corrections in your story.

3. Submit your story to your teacher for further comments and corrections.

4. Read your story to the class.

# 7. Reading Work Schedules

**A** Read the supermarket work schedule with a partner.

| WORK SCHEDULE: WEEK OF APRIL 10–16 | | | | | | | |
|---|---|---|---|---|---|---|---|
| Name | Mon. | Tues. | Wed. | Thurs. | Fri. | Sat. | Sun. |
| Suzy | 6 A.M.–2:30 P.M.* | 7 A.M.–3:30 P.M.* | 7 A.M.–3:30 P.M.* | —— | 6 A.M.–2:30 P.M.* | —— | 8 A.M.–4:30 P.M.* |
| Juan | 2–6 P.M. | 2–6 P.M. | 3–7 P.M. | 6–9 P.M. | 4–8 P.M. | —— | 4–8 P.M. |
| Mayra | 1–9:30 P.M.* | 1–9:30 P.M.* | 2–10:30 P.M.* | 2–10:30 P.M.* | —— | 2–10:30 P.M.* | —— |
| Ray | 10 P.M.–6:30 A.M.* | —— | 10 A.M.–6:30 P.M.* | 10 A.M.–6:30 P.M.* | —— | 10 A.M.–6:30 P.M.* | 10 A.M.–6:30 P.M.* |
| Kim | 4–10 P.M.* | 1–9:30 P.M.* | —— | 4–10:30 P.M.* | —— | 4–10:30 P.M.* | 4–10:30 P.M.* |

**\*includes 30-minute meal break**

*(continued on next page)*

**B** Answer these questions about the schedule.

1. Which days and hours does Mayra work? Which are her days off?

   _____

2. Who works full time (40 hours) at the market? _____

   _____

3. Who works part time (fewer than 40 hours)? _____

   _____

4. Which workers have a shift of 6 hours or more and should be scheduled for a meal break? _____

★5. Why is it important for employees to read the work schedule?

   _____

★6. For what other types of jobs could the work schedule change from day to day?

   _____

# 8. Getting Paid

**A** Read the story.

▲ ATM Machine

## Direct Deposit

My name is Mark Hathaway. I work for Amco Rental Trucks as a driver. My payday is Thursday. The company has a program they call direct deposit. This means they transfer money into my bank account electronically. Then I can get the money from the cash machine at 6:00 P.M. on my payday.

I like direct deposit because I don't have to worry that my money will be lost. I don't have to go to the bank to deposit my check. It saves me time, and it's very safe.

**B** Talk about these questions in a group. Write your answer.
What does *automatic* or *direct deposit* mean?

_____

What are two things Mark likes about direct deposit?

_____

**C** Discuss the following questions with the class.

1. What are different ways to be paid? Which do you prefer?
2. Where can checks be cashed or deposited?
3. What identification is needed to cash a check?

# 9. Situations—Paychecks, Pay Stubs, and Deductions

**A** Read each section of the pay stub below.

| EMPLOYEE NAME | ADAN SILANO | | DESCRIPTION | DEDUCTIONS (This pay period) | YEAR-TO-DATE | TOTAL GROSS PAY | TOTAL NET PAY |
|---|---|---|---|---|---|---|---|
| EMPLOYEE NUMBER | 43099 | | FEDERAL TAX | 30.00 | 60.00 | | |
| PAY PERIOD | 1/19/98–1/30/98 | | STATE TAX | .20 | .40 | | |
| AMOUNT OF CHECK | 635.84 | | FICA | 39.68 | 79.36 | | |
| | | | MEDICARE | 9.28 | 18.56 | | |
| DESCRIPTION | HOURS | PAY RATE | MEDICAL INSURANCE | 49.00 | 98.00 | | |
| REGULAR | 80 | 8.20 | UNION DUES | 15.00 | 30.00 | | |
| OVERTIME | 10 | 12.30 | | | | | |
| YEAR-TO-DATE | REGULAR | 1312.00 | YEAR-TO-DATE GROSS | | 1558.00 | | |
| YEAR-TO-DATE | OVERTIME | 246.00 | YEAR-TO-DATE NET | | 1271.88 | 779.00 | 635.84 |

**B** With your class, read the information about pay stubs and deductions.

## Work Culture Notes: Pay Stub

The pay stub section of your paycheck **itemizes** your pay and all the deductions from your pay. When you receive your check, deductions should already have been taken from it. Always review your pay stub to make sure it is accurate.

| | |
|---|---|
| **Gross Pay** | Pay before deductions |
| **Net Pay** | Money after deductions |
| **Regular Pay** | Pay that is not overtime pay |
| **Overtime Pay** | Extra pay for more than 40 hours worked per week |
| **Pay period** | Time period covered by the check |

**Deductions**   Money taken out of your check
  **Federal Withholding Tax**   Money taken out by the U.S. government
  **FICA**   (Federal Insurance Contributions Act) Money used for Social Security
  **State Withholding Tax**   Money taken out by the state government
  **Health/Medical Insurance**   Money taken out for medical care
  **Union Dues**   Money deducted for union membership

**C** Review the check stub in 9A. Answer these questions.

1. What was the pay period of the check? _____

2. How many regular hours and how many overtime hours were worked? _____

3. What was the gross pay? _____

4. What deductions were taken out? _____
_____

5. How much was deducted for Social Security? _____
for state and federal taxes? _____

6. What do union dues cover? _____

7. What was the pay after deductions (net pay)? _____

**D** Solve these pay problems.

1. Teresa's pay as a hostess at Stevens Brothers' Restaurant is $6.50 per hour. Last week she worked 40 regular hours and 2 hours of overtime (overtime is 1½ times regular pay).

   What is her gross pay? _____

2. Leonard works at the post office as a clerk. His pay is $18.00 per hour. In the last pay period he was paid for 72 hours regular time, 8 hours of **sick pay**, and 8 hours of overtime.

   What is his gross pay? _____

3. From Sonya's weekly check of $700.00 these amounts are deducted:

   FICA (Social Security) _____ *43.40* _____

   Federal tax _____ *105.00* _____

   State taxes _____ *53.55* _____

   Medicare _____ *10.15* _____

   Medical insurance _____ *45.00* _____

   What is Sonya's net pay? _____

**Definition**

sick pay
wages
paid to
workers
who are
sick

---

**E** Listen to the conversation. Write the kind of deduction on the line.

1. _____

2. _____

3. _____

4. _____

# 10. Understanding Labor Laws

**A** Work with your partner. Read the information on the poster.

**Work Culture Notes: Know Your Rights:**

## The Fair Labor Standards Act

### Federal Minimum Wage
### is
### $5.15 per hour

**The Federal Labor Standards Act** sets the **minimum wage** for most workers at $5.15 per hour. The minimum wage means the lowest amount an employer can pay a worker per hour. (There are special restrictions on the work of children under the age of 16 and special provisions for students and workers who earn tips.)

**Overtime Pay**   At least 1½ times your regular rate of pay for all the hours worked over 40 in a work week.

**Enforcement**   The U.S. Department of Labor may **recover back wages,** either administratively or through court action, for employees who have been **underpaid** in violation of the law. Violations may result in civil or criminal action. Fines of up to $1,000 per violation may be assessed against employers who violate the minimum wage and overtime provisions.

## Definitions

**minimum wage**
the lowest legal amount an employer must pay a worker

**recover** to get back

**back wages** money owed to a worker by a company

**underpaid** to be paid less than what you are owed or you have earned

**B** Answer the questions.

1. Which law establishes the federal minimum wage?

_____

2. What is the federal minimum wage? $_____ per hour

3. What does *minimum* mean? _____

_____

4. To whom does the law apply? _____

5. What does the U.S. Department of Labor do to enforce the law?

_____

**C** Find out the minimum wage in your state. You may call the library, ask an employer, or call your state department of labor. (The minimum wage in your state may be higher than the federal minimum wage.) Find out which jobs pay minimum wage and which pay more. List the information in the chart below.

| FEDERAL MINIMUM WAGE | STATE MINIMUM WAGE |
| --- | --- |
| **JOBS PAYING MINIMUM WAGE** | **JOBS PAYING MORE THAN MINIMUM WAGE** |
|  |  |
|  |  |
|  |  |
|  |  |

**D** With your teacher and class, discuss a job in which workers are paid less than minimum wage. How much are they paid? Why do you think they are paid below minimum wage? What would you suggest they do about the problem? Why do you think some jobs pay minimum wage and some pay more?

With a partner, write a story about workers who are paid less than minimum wage. Use the questions above to help your thinking.

## 11. Vocabulary and Information Game

Sit in a group of four. Your group will need one die and each student will need a marker. Throw the die, move your marker around the gameboard and answer the question you land on. If you do not know an answer, go back to your previous square.

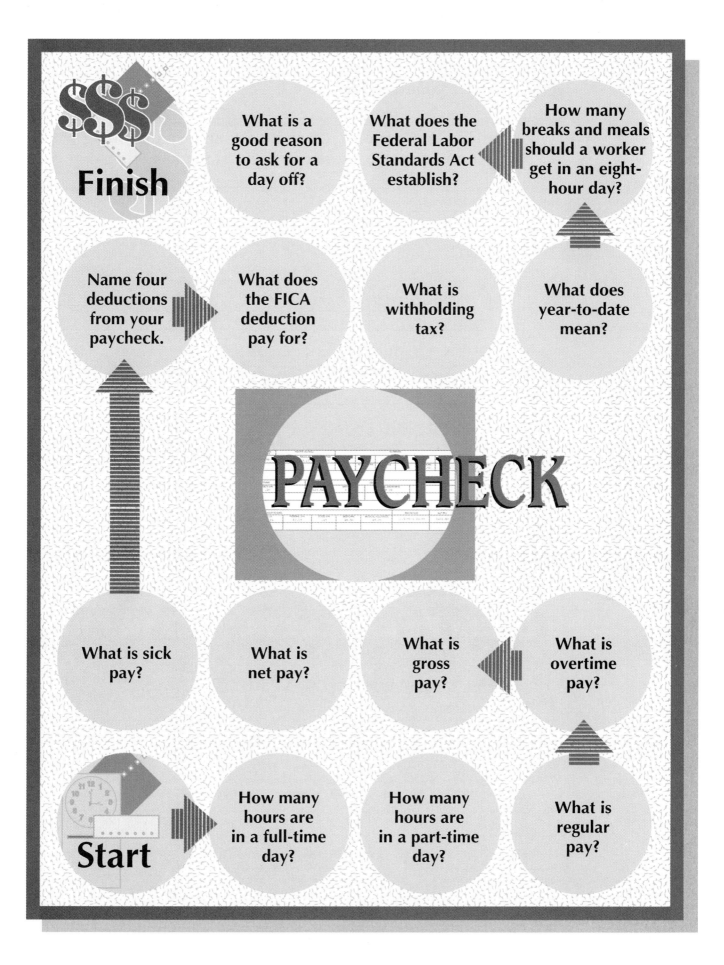

**Finish**

What is a good reason to ask for a day off?

What does the Federal Labor Standards Act establish?

How many breaks and meals should a worker get in an eight-hour day?

Name four deductions from your paycheck.

What does the FICA deduction pay for?

What is withholding tax?

What does year-to-date mean?

**PAYCHECK**

What is sick pay?

What is net pay?

What is gross pay?

What is overtime pay?

**Start**

How many hours are in a full-time day?

How many hours are in a part-time day?

What is regular pay?

## 12. Assessing Your Progress

**A** 1. Describe your daily schedule. _____

_____

2. Name an unacceptable reason for asking for a day off.
   Name an acceptable reason for asking for a day off.

_____

_____

3. What is overtime work? At what rate should overtime work
   be paid?

_____

4. What does *direct deposit* mean? _____

_____

5. What is a pay stub? _____

6. Name four deductions from your paycheck. _____

_____   _____   _____

7. What do the labor laws in this state say about breaks? about meals?

_____

_____

8. What is the federal law concerning the minimum wage?

_____

_____

## 13. Looking Back

| **A** Things I learned about work schedules and paychecks | How I can apply what I learned to my life |
|---|---|
| 1. | |
| 2. | |
| 3. | |
| **B** New words and idioms | Related words from my job |
| 1. | |
| 2. | |
| 3. | |

# 7 SAFETY

## 1. Talking About Work

▲ **Look at the picture. Discuss these questions with your teacher and class.**

**Definition**

**fumes** gas, smoke, or smell, often from a chemical

▶ What are the two workers doing?

▶ Why do you think the man with the painter's cap needs some air?

▶ What should the workers wear to protect themselves from chemical **fumes**?

★ ▶ Who is responsible for safety in the workplace?

★ ▶ Are there laws that require a safe and healthy work environment? What are they?

## 2. Work Stories

**A** Discuss the words with your teacher and classmates. Write your ideas on the lines.

safety          accidents

**B** Read

▲ Rodolfo Hernandez

### Definitions

**hurried** rushed

**safety measures** procedures to avoid accidents

**productivity** the amount of work done in a limited time

**stocker** person who loads and unloads items and puts them on the shelf

### Reading Strategy: Preview

Before you read the story:

1. Read the title.
2. Look at the picture.
3. Read the first sentence of each paragraph.
4. Read the last paragraph.
5. Talk about these questions:
   a. What do you think the story is about?
   b. What do you already know about safety at work?

**Hurry Up!** by Rodolfo Hernandez

As long as I can remember, working means being **hurried**. Don't get me wrong, I love to work. I'm proud that I've always found ways to get the job done faster. Unfortunately, it has been at the expense of my health. I think that some companies set aside **safety measures** in order to increase the **productivity** of their employees. Here is my example.

I worked for almost five years as a **stocker** at a supermarket. I used to work the night shift. My coworkers and I moved boxes from the back room to the store aisles. Then we put the products on the shelves.

When the managers realized that my two coworkers and I could do the same work as seven people, they reduced the hours of the slower ones. They made the three of us do the work of seven. As a result, we had to work faster and harder.

Sometimes one of us had to pull heavy loads of merchandise without a forklift. With only three people, we couldn't work together. My back was always aching because there weren't enough of us to pull the **pallets.**

To be safe at work, I believe that both employees and employers have to take safety matters seriously. Unfortunately my experience was with a company that always told us: Hurry up! Hurry up!

## 3. Thinking About the Story

**A** Talk about these questions with a partner.

1. What does a supermarket stocker do?
2. Why did the store manager reduce the hours of the slower workers?
3. What do you think Rodolfo means when he says, "working means being hurried"?
4. What safety measures did the managers **overlook?** Why?
★ 5. What do you think the results will be of Rodolfo pulling heavy pallet loads by himself?

**B** Read Rodolfo's story again. With your partner, write seven questions (who, what, where, when, why, how long, and how many) about the story. After you finish, ask your teacher to check your questions.

***Example:*** *Where* did Rodolfo work?

Pick four students and four of your questions. Ask each student one question. When you finish with one student, move to another student and ask a different question.

**C** As a class, retell Rodolfo's story. Each person adds one sentence. Continue until the story is finished. Then tell the story again to your partner.

★ **D** In his story Rodolfo says that the increase in his **workload** created a safety problem. Talk about these questions.

Why do companies increase a person's workload?

What kind of health problems can develop when a workload is increased?

What could the company do to prevent worker health problems?

What could Rodolfo do to prevent potential health problems?

**E** Read the story again. Circle any new words. Add these words to the **work dictionary** in your notebook or to the vocabulary database in your computer. Write the meaning next to each word. Use it in a sentence.

| Word | Meaning | Sentence |
|------|---------|----------|
| *hurry* | to move faster | The mechanic hurried to fix the car before the garage closed. |

# 4. After the Story

**A** Read.

## Work Culture Notes: Health and Safety

### The Occupational Safety and Health Act of 1970

*Working Conditions:* The Occupational Safety and Health Act requires employers to provide safe jobs and healthy working conditions for workers. All workplaces must be free from **health hazards** that can be dangerous to employees. These include dust, fumes, chemicals that cause disease, machinery with no **guards,** high noise levels, electrical wiring problems, and equipment problems.

*Complaint and Inspection:* If employees believe that a workplace is unsafe, they may file a **complaint** with **OSHA.** They request an inspection of the workplace by an inspector.

*Corrections and Fines:* After an OSHA inspection, if the OSHA inspector finds an employer has violated the Occupational Safety and Health Act, the employer must correct the problems. If the employer does not correct the problems, he or she may have to pay a **fine** of up to $7,000 for each violation.

### Definitions

**health hazard** something dangerous to your health

**guard** protection on a machine

**complaint** criticism

**OSHA** Occupational Safety and Health Administration, a section of the U.S. Department of Labor

**fine** money paid for breaking the law

**B** Think about a job and the safety and health conditions on the job. Your teacher will read these questions. Write your answers. If you are not sure, write "not sure". Then ask a partner the questions and write down his or her answers.

| | You | Your Partner |
|---|---|---|
| **1.** What is the job? | | |
| **2.** What do workers wear to protect themselves? | | |
| **3.** What machines are dangerous? Why? | | |
| **4.** What chemicals can be dangerous? Why? | | |
| **5.** What working conditions exist that can be dangerous to workers' health? | | |

**C** Work with a team. Describe an accident or a health problem you had at work or at home. What was the cause of the accident? How could it have been prevented? What can you do to prevent it from happening again?

**D** Many companies have a safety committee. With your team, select a work problem from 4C. Write a memo explaining the problem. Make recommendations for creating a safer workplace.

Your teacher will ask some groups to read their memos to the class.

To: Safety Committee
From:
Date:
Subject: Safety and Health Problem

_____ is a health and safety problem at our workplace.

(Give some examples why it is a problem.) _____

_____

_____

To solve this problem we think the company should:

1)

2)

We would like to talk with you about this problem as soon as possible.

Sincerely yours,

_____  _____  _____
(team members' signatures)

# 5. Safety Inventory

**A** Safety rules exist on every job. Pair up with a person who is currently working (if you are working, pair up with someone who isn't). Make a check (✔) next to all the rules that apply to your job or your partner's job.

_____ **1.** Wear a hair net.
_____ **2.** Sit in a good chair with back support.
_____ **3.** Store materials out of aisles and loading areas.
_____ **4.** Read all **warning labels** before handling chemicals or hazardous substances.
_____ **5.** Wear necessary **Personal Protective Equipment (PPE):** ear plugs, ear muffs, apron, safety shoes, back support belt, gloves, face mask, hard hat, goggles, or respirator.
_____ **6.** Clean up any accidental **spills** or leaks.
_____ **7.** Wash your hands with soap and water before handling food.
_____ **8.** Unplug machines before repairing them.
_____ **9.** Always **lift** safely. Bend from the knees. Bring the load to your body and lift using your leg muscles.
_____ **10.** Wear a seat belt when operating a car, truck, or forklift.
_____ **11.** Check all tools and equipment before using them to make sure they are in good condition.
_____ **12.** Don't smoke.
_____ **13.** Don't wear ties, long sleeves, loose-fitting clothing, or jewelry.
_____ **14.** Use a protective screen over the computer monitor to prevent eye strain.
_____ **15.** Wear a mask to protect yourself from breathing in dust.
_____ **16.** Before you start a machine, make sure the guards are in place.
_____ **17.** Read all safety signs.
_____ **18.** Notify a supervisor of any **defective** tools or equipment.
_____ **19.** Notify a supervisor immediately of all work accidents and injuries.
_____ **20.** Always wear closed-toed shoes. Never wear sandals or shoes without socks.

## Definitions

**warning label** information about the danger of a product

**PPE** safety clothing

**spill** to cause liquid to fall out of its container

**lift** to pick up

**defective** not working correctly

**B** Review the safety rules listed in 5A in a group. Next to each rule write the categories that it applies to (food service, office work, construction, factory work), or write G for general rule.

**Examples:** _food_ **1.** Wear a hair net.
_G_ **17.** Read all safety signs.

**C** Choose five of the above rules. Explain to your group members why each rule is important.

# 6. Work Safety Problem

**A** Read the story.

▲ Gelacio Chay

## Definitions

**scrape off** to remove

**rust** reddish coating on metal caused by air and moisture

**Safety Equipment** by Gelacio Chay

I work in an auto body shop. I paint cars 40 hours a week. Working as a car painter is very hard and dangerous. We use many chemicals, such as thinner, primer, paint, lacquer, and enamel hardener.

To prepare each car, I sand down the old paint and **scrape off** the **rust**. There is a lot of dust. Later, I move the car into the spray area. This is where we paint cars with a spray gun. The chemicals are very strong. We apply six coats of paint.

When I first started working in this body shop, the boss didn't supply me with any safety equipment. He just wanted me to finish the job. When I finished painting, my nose and throat felt full of paint. I had a headache, I was dizzy, and I lost my coordination.

Then a friend at work told me what could happen if I didn't use the necessary safety equipment. He told me what to buy: a face mask, goggles, a protective suit to cover my clothes, and safety shoes. The mask was the most important. I bought the equipment myself. Because I did that, I don't have any problems now. I recommend you always wear the necessary equipment to do this job or any job.

When you are twenty-five years old, you feel young and strong. You don't feel the effect of the chemicals on your body. But when you're older and you have worked for many years, your body really feels it. You get headaches and you are dizzy, you feel tired, have sore throats and have problems breathing through your nose.

I bought my own safety equipment that first time. Now I know better. When I need to replace my equipment, I tell my boss what I need and he buys it for me.

**B** What safety equipment did Gelacio need to wear on his job? Why?

1. *goggles, to protect his eyes* _____

2. _____

3. _____

4. _____

**C** Discuss these questions.

    **1.** Why do you think the boss didn't buy Gelacio the necessary equipment at first?

    **2.** What do you think Gelacio meant about the difference between younger workers and older workers?

   ⋆ **3.** Why do you think the boss changed his mind and decided to buy Gelacio the necessary equipment?

# 7. Understanding the Workplace

**A** Work in a group. Imagine that you work in the shipping department of an appliance manufacturing company. There is a problem with the **ventilation** system. Listen to the conversation. With your teammates, discuss the questions.

*Questions:*
    What problem is Victor reporting?
    Does Mr. Schilling think there is a heating problem?
    What did Victor request that Mr. Schilling do about the problem?
    What was Mr. Shilling's response?
    What do you think will happen?

**Definition**

ventilation a system to move air in a room

**B** Practice requesting help with health and safety problems at work.

### Requesting Help

    **1.** *Would you* check our department for chemical fumes and dust in the air?

    **2.** *Could you* have a maintenance supervisor check the ventilation?

For more practice with **requesting help**, turn to the **Grammar Appendix**.

**C** Work in a group of four. Listen to each speaker. Then discuss what each individual or group can do. Act out each situation in your group or in front of your class.

    **1.** What can they do?

      **a.** Smile and keep working. Be happy to have a job.
      **b.** Buy their own heaters and fans.
      **c.** Write a memo to the safety committee. Then meet with the committee to discuss the problem.
      **d.** Refuse to work until the ventilator is repaired.

2. What can the speaker do?
   a. Bring in his own lamp.
   b. Check with the manager. Get a definite date when the lights will be replaced.
   c. Call in sick every day until the lights are replaced.
   d. Ask to move to another space.

3. What can she do?
   a. Say nothing, because she might lose her job.
   b. Continue working. Ask another worker to do any heavy work for her.
   c. Report the accident to the supervisor and go to the medical clinic.
   d. Quit her job to recover from her back injury.

4. What can she do?
   a. Talk to her coworkers and see if they have the same problem.
   b. Quit and look for a different job.
   c. Not say anything and hope it goes away.
   d. Discuss the problem with her coworkers and then with her supervisor.

 ⋆ **D** Your team members report health and safety problems. Talk about each problem and the reason for the problem. Then suggest a solution. Add one problem you are familiar with to the chart.

> ***Example:*** **Problem:** Workers can't see warning labels on boxes.
> **Possible solution:** "You *could* install additional lighting."

| PROBLEM | REASON FOR THE PROBLEM | POSSIBLE SOLUTION |
| --- | --- | --- |
| workers can't see warning labels on boxes | not enough lighting | *install additional lighting* |
| workers have backaches | bending down and lifting heavy boxes | |
| workers have breathing problems | chemical fumes in the air | |
| workers slip and fall on wet floors | water spills | |
| worker can't hear instructions from supervisors | high noise level | |
| | | |

**Definition**

injury  a
wound or
damage
to the
body

# 8. Understanding Work Graphs and Injury Reports

**A** A medium-sized factory that makes large airplane parts reported these on-the-job **injuries**. The machines in the factory are computerized. Read the information on the line graph.

Injuries to the Body: 1990 to the Present

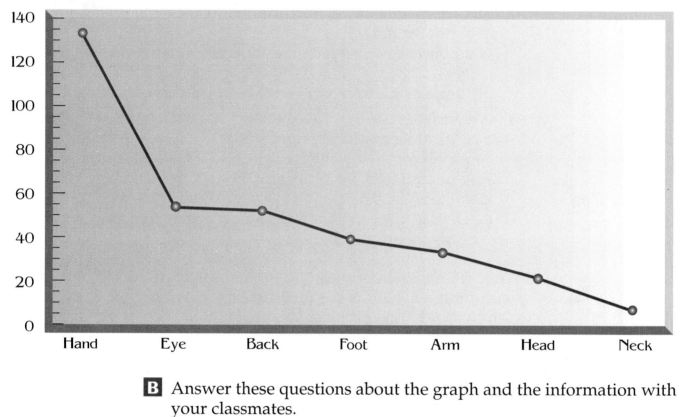

**B** Answer these questions about the graph and the information with your classmates.

1. What years does the graph cover ? _____

2. To which part of the body did the most injuries occur? How many?

   _____

3. To which part of the body did the fewest injuries occur? How many?

   _____

★**4.** Why do you think there were so many injuries to the hands?

   _____

   _____

★**5.** What can the factory safety committee and the union safety committee recommend to prevent additional injuries to the hands? _____

   _____

**C** Survey your class. Make a line graph of the accidents or injuries that students from the class have had at home or on the job.

**D** Yevgeny works in the cutting department. At 7:00 A.M. on January 15 he cut his left hand. He was using an electric saw. The guard in front of the saw blade was not down and the machine was on. He was holding the metal and his fingers got too close to the saw blade. He wasn't wearing any protective equipment at the time. The accident happened in Department 5. Fill out the Industrial Injury and Illness Report.

## Industrial Injury and Illness Report

**Instructions: Please fill this form out within 24 hours of the injury. State the facts accurately. Turn it in to the safety coordinator.**

Employee's Name _____ Department _____

Date of injury or illness: _____ Time _____ A.M. _____ P.M.

Place of injury or illness: _____

Part(s) of body injured: _____

Description of injury or illness: _____

_____

What was the employee doing when the accident occurred? _____

_____

_____

Was safety equipment being used at the time? _____

_____

Were all guards in place at the time of the injury? If no, explain why. _____

_____

_____

_____

Describe how the injury happened. _____

_____

_____

_____

What could have been done to prevent the injury? _____

_____

_____

_____

Employee Signature _____ Date _____

Supervisor Signature _____ Date _____

**E** Discuss these questions with your group and then with the entire class.

**1.** Why is it necessary to immediately report all accidents to a supervisor?

**2.** Why is it necessary to immediately send injured workers to the medical clinic?

**3.** Why is it necessary for a company to have a written report of all on-the-job accidents?

★ **4.** Why is it necessary for a company to keep statistics on the number and kind of accidents and injuries?

## 9. Listening at Work: Safety Goals

You are listening to an end-of-year safety meeting. Mary Reynolds, Safety Coordinator, is speaking to supervisors and safety representatives from every department. Listen to the information and take notes. Record the information in the chart.

**1.** Total injuries and accidents (not more than) _____

**2.** Accident investigation reports (completed within) _____

**3.** Safety meetings (how many) _____

**4.** Machine safety (completed by) _____

**5.** Personal protective equipment (who must wear; what happens if they don't) _____

_____

**6.** Training classes (when and for what) _____

_____

## 10. Workplace Vocabulary

**A** Fill in the following sentences using the workplace vocabulary words. Compare your answers with your classmates. Then find the pages where the words are used in the chapter and fill in the page numbers.

| | | | | |
|---|---|---|---|---|
| fine | safety equipment | lifted | label | spills |
| health hazard | OSHA | workload | fumes | guard |

**Page Number**

**1.** _____ is a government agency   _____
that checks on working conditions.

2. An open chemical container may be a     _____

   _____ _____.

3. The Acme Company refused to repair their     _____
   broken machines after a report by an OSHA
   inspector. They had to pay a _____
   of $7,000.

4. The warehouse worker bent her knees and     _____
   _____ the box.

5. Be sure to read the warning _____     _____
   before working with chemicals.

6. Before Zhou started to use the machine, he     _____
   checked to see if the _____
   was in place.

7. Mika's _____ was to sew more than     _____
   200 dresses a day.

8. Always wear the necessary _____     _____
   _____. It will help protect you
   from injury and illness on the job.

9. You can't always see chemical _____,     _____
   but they are still dangerous.

10. Clean up _____ from the     _____
    floor immediately.

**B** Select two words from the vocabulary list. Write each word on a
piece of paper. Ask one student to give a definition of one word
and to use the word in a sentence. Then ask another student to
define the second word and use it in a sentence.

## 11. Assessing Your Progress

**A** Write your answers to the following questions.

1. What federal agency monitors safety and health conditions
   on-the-job?

   _____

2. What are four examples of safety equipment?

   _____  _____

   _____  _____

3. What are three examples of health hazards?

   _____

   _____

   _____

**4.** Name three job safety rules.

_____

_____

_____

**5.** What two things should you do if you have a work accident?

_____     _____

**6.** What form do you fill out with a supervisor when there is a work accident?

_____

**7.** Why is it necessary to report all work accidents to the supervisor immediately?

_____

**8.** What does a work safety committee do?

_____

**9.** Give an example of how you plan to work more safely on your job in the future.

_____

## 12. Looking Back

| **A** Things I learned about health and safety at work | How I can apply what I learned to my life |
|---|---|
| 1. | |
| 2. | |
| 3. | |
| **B** New words and idioms | Related words from my job |
| 1. | |
| 2. | |
| 3. | |

# 8 LABOR UNIONS, LABOR LAWS, AND BENEFITS

## 1. Talking About Work

▲ **Look at the picture. Discuss these questions with your teacher and class.**

> ▶ What do you think the people are discussing?
> ▶ What is a union?
> ▶ What are some benefits that workers have if they belong to a union?
> ★ ▶ How do union representatives negotiate with company representatives?

# 2. Work Stories

**A** Discuss these words with your teacher and classmates. Write your ideas on the lines.

_____ } **labor unions** { _____

_____ } { _____

**B** Read

▲ Yvonne Nishio

## Reading Strategy: Predict True and False

Before you read the story, read the following sentences. For each, write **T** if you think it is true, **F** if you think it is false.

1. A teachers' union is a small organization.
2. A union protects its members.
3. Pay and benefits can be guaranteed in a union contract.
4. A strike can have no good results.

Now read the story to see if your predictions are correct.

### Definitions

**favoritism** treating some people better than others

**minority** any person from a group that is not more than 50 percent of the total population

**contract** written agreement between a labor union and a company or organization

## Union Member by Yvonne Nishio

I've been a member of United Teachers of Los Angeles, UTLA, the teachers' union, for 30 years. There are 32,000 members of our union working in more than 600 schools. I'm proud to be a member of this union because it protects all the teachers in our school district. In UTLA, the membership is active in making decisions.

For many years, schools didn't have enough classrooms and materials for the growing number of students. We want to meet the needs of our students. The union has helped us get support and money for public education. Our union makes our students' needs known to administrators, politicians, and voters.

Thirty years ago, not all teachers were represented by the union. Administrators used a lot of **favoritism**. They selected their favorite teachers and gave them the best assignments and extra pay. Frequently, **minority** teachers were made to work in poorer neighborhoods. With our union **contract**, things have changed a lot. Our contract

**guarantees** our right to equal pay, equal benefits, and equal treatment on the job. Union members receive the same pay for the same work. There can be no discrimination.

The union contract also protects us from being unfairly **laid off** or **fired.** Our contract says that teachers can only be laid off in order of **seniority.** If a class is canceled, the last teacher hired is the first teacher to be laid off.

In 1989, we went out on **strike** for five days. The two most important issues were higher pay for teachers and having teachers involved in school decision making. We stopped teaching and walked on a **picket** line. As a result of the strike, teachers got higher pay and school councils were formed so that teachers could be involved in school decision making.

# 3. Thinking About the Story

**A** Read the story again. Write a complete sentence to state the main idea of each paragraph. Work with a group.

1. *Yvonne is a member of a large and active teachers' union.*

2. _____

3. _____

4. _____

5. _____

**B** Unions provide workers with many benefits and protections. Which does Yvonne talk about in her story? Work with a partner. Write your answers on the lines.

*equal pay for all workers* _____

_____  _____

★ **C** Do you think Yvonne's teaching job is better because she is in a union? Discuss your opinion in a group. Share it with your class.

**D** Read the story again. Circle any new words. Add these words to the **work dictionary** in your notebook or to the vocabulary database in your computer. Write the meaning next to each word. Use it in a sentence.

| Word | Meaning | Sentence |
|------|---------|----------|
| *union* | an organization that represents workers | The members of the union met to talk about workers' problems. |

# 4. After the Story

**A** **Work Culture Notes: Labor Unions**

**Purpose:** A union is an organization representing a group of working people. The union helps working people protect their **rights.**

**Contract:** The rights and benefits to union members are guaranteed in the union contract. These rights and benefits can include pay, safe working conditions, hours of work, job security, promotions, benefits, protection against discrimination, and job education and training. The union contract is signed by representatives of the company and the union.

**Definitions**

**rights** permission to do something guaranteed by law

**grievance** a written complaint

**Grievance:** If a union member has a disagreement with a boss, she or he may file a **grievance.**

**Representation:** When there is a disagreement in the workplace involving a union member, a union representative may speak for the union member.

**Members:** Union members are women and men, people of all races, religions, nationalities, and sexual preferences. There can be no discrimination in union membership.

**Dues:** Union members pay money every month to cover the costs of the union.

**General Information:** According to one survey in 1988, of 101,700,000 workers in the United States, 17,002,000, or 17 percent, were union members.

**B** Review the **Work Culture Notes** and the story. Answer these questions. Discuss your answers with your teacher and classmates.

1. What is a labor union?
2. What does a union representative do?
3. What is a union contract?
4. What is a strike?
5. How can a union protect its members from discrimination and harassment?

**C** Invite a union member or representative to talk to your class. Find out the following information. What other questions would you like to ask?

Name of the union _____

Number of union members _____

Work the members do _____

Pay of members of this union _____

Benefits and protections for union members _____

_____

Union dues _____

General membership meetings _____

History of the union (when and why the union was formed) _____

_____

_____

**D** What did you find out about the union? Review the information with your classmates.

**E** Write a letter to the union representative. Thank her or him for visiting your class. (Type the letter on the word processing program in your computer.)

(your address)
(your city)

(date)

(name of person)
(name of union)
(address of union)

Dear _____:

    Thank you for speaking to our class about the _____ union.

I learned several things from your talk. _____

_____

_____

I would like to have more information about _____.

    It was a pleasure to have you visit our class.

Sincerely yours,

(your signature)

# 5. Personal History and Unions

**A** Work in a group. Some of the students in the group should have union experience.

Discuss these questions.

1. How are unions in the United States similar to unions in your country?
2. How are unions in the United States different from unions in your country?
3. Were you ever in a union in your country?
4. Has a union ever helped you? What happened?
5. Are there any disadvantages to being a union member? If so, what are they?

**B** Use your answers in 5A to help you write.

1. In your notebook, make a list of your ideas.
2. Select one question from 5A. Describe to a classmate your experience or the experience of someone you know with unions.
3. Your partner will suggest additional information you could add to make your story more interesting.
4. Write a story using your ideas.
5. Read your story to your partner. Your partner will suggest ways to make your story clearer.

★ **C** Continue the writing process.

1. Another partner will check your story and make suggestions for punctuation and correct verbs. You will do the same for him or her.
2. Make the corrections in your story.
3. Read your story to the class.
4. Submit your story to your teacher for further correction and comment.

# 6. Discrimination and Equal Rights Protections

**A** Several U.S. federal laws protect the rights of all working people. Read the descriptions.

| | |
|---|---|
| **1.** Equal Pay Act of 1963 | –No discrimination in pay to women or men performing the same work |
| **2.** Civil Rights Act of 1964 | –No discrimination in hiring, pay, promotion, layoffs, benefits, or training on the basis of race, color, religion, sex, or nationality<br>–No discrimination on the basis of pregnancy |
| **3.** Age Discrimination in Employment Act of 1967 | –No discrimination in hiring, pay, promotion, layoffs, and conditions of employment for employees age 40 and over |
| **4.** Americans with Disabilities Act of 1990 | –No discrimination in hiring, pay, promotion, layoffs, benefits, or training on the basis of disability |
| **5.** National Labor Relations Act | –Gives employees the right to organize and **bargain collectively** with employers |
| **6.** Family Medical Leave Act of 1993 | –Allows worker to take a **leave** for personal or family medical problems |

**Definitions**

**bargain collectively** negotiate in a group

**leave** time away from work

**B** Work in a group of four. Listen to each speaker. Then discuss the kind of discrimination experienced, the law violated, and what each person can do.

1. What kind of discrimination did Goi report? What additional information do you need to investigate the problem? Was a law violated? What do you suggest she do?

2. What kind of discrimination did Samuel report? What additional information do you need to investigate the problem? Was a law violated? What do you suggest he do?

3. What kind of discrimination did Olga report? What additional information do you need to investigate the problem? Was a law violated? What do you suggest she do?

4. What kind of discrimination did Esther report? What additional information do you need to investigate the problem? Was a law violated? What do you suggest the older man do?

**C** Review each situation in 6B. What would you advise each person to do?

**D** In a team, discuss examples of discrimination that happened to you or someone you know. Each person has two minutes to talk.

★ **E** Talk with a partner about this question: Have you ever discriminated against another person? What did you do? What did the other person do? What happened?

# 7. Work Benefits

**A** Read the story.

▲ Sujan Guo

**What I Like About My Job** by Sujan Guo

I have been working as a teacher's aide for the last two years for the City College of San Francisco. I work with students in the Literacy and Citizenship programs. Sometimes I prepare students for citizenship exams. I also tutor individual students, assist students with group and pair practice, and help teachers prepare their materials. I love my work.

Nowadays it is difficult for a new immigrant to find a job, if he or she can find one at all. I am in a union and I have good benefits. My benefits are limited because I work only part time. My benefits include medical insurance, six paid holidays a year, and six sick days per year. I also get retirement benefits. These are very good benefits. However, if I were working full time, 40 hours a week, I would also get vacation pay, dental insurance, vision insurance, and life insurance.

On this job I have met so many wonderful and devoted teachers. It is always fun for me to work and study together with the teachers and the students. I sincerely hope that my efforts to teach and tutor my students will help them to achieve a better future.

**B** Discuss these questions with a partner.

1. Does Sujan work full time or part time?
2. What benefits does Sujan receive on her job?
3. What other benefits would she receive if she worked 40 hours (full time)?

**C** Sujan discusses eight possible benefits. Circle the types of benefits in her story. Take turns with your partner thinking of a job. Ask your partner questions about the benefits on the job; then your partner will ask you questions.

*Example:* Is there medical insurance on your job?

**D** Discuss this question in a group: Which benefits (from those in the story) are the most important for you and your family? Why? Make a list showing your first priority, second priority, and so on.

_____   _____   _____

_____   _____   _____

## 8. Understanding the Workplace: Full Time and Part Time Work

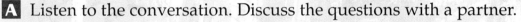

**A** Listen to the conversation. Discuss the questions with a partner.

*Questions:*
What is Sayeed's problem?
Did Mr. Chang offer him a full-time job?
What did the employer suggest about the future?
What do you think will happen?
★ Is it a good idea to ask a boss for more hours? more pay? more overtime? Why?

**B** Practice asking and answering these questions about an employee's job.

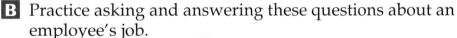

GRAMMAR

*Asking about a period of time*

| **Employer** | **Employee** |
|---|---|
| *How long have you been* working for this company? | I've been working here *for* three years. |
| *How long have you been* working part time? | *Since* I was hired two years ago. |
| *How long have you been* working as a cook? | I've been working as a cook *for* five years. |

For more help **asking about a period of time,** turn to the **Grammar Appendix.**

**C** Many companies use part-time workers. With your teammates, brainstorm a list of jobs in which most people work part time.

*fast-food restaurants* _____ _____

_____ _____ _____

_____ _____ _____

Why do you think some industries hire so many part-time workers?

**D** What are the advantages and disadvantages of working part time? Discuss this question with your teammates. Write your answers on the lines.

| ADVANTAGES | DISADVANTAGES |
|---|---|
| *flexible hours* | *limited benefits* |
| | |
| | |
| | |

**E** Survey your class. Ask each student whether he or she wants to work part time or full time. Record the totals in the chart. Calculate the percentages.

| | TOTALS | PERCENTAGE OF CLASS |
|---|---|---|
| Want part-time work | | |
| Want full-time work | | |

# 9. Medical Benefits

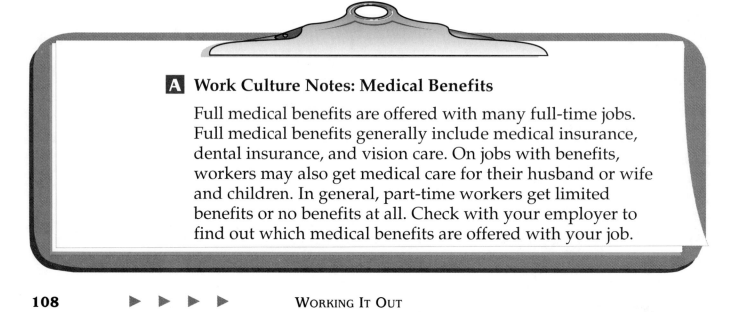

**A** Work Culture Notes: Medical Benefits

Full medical benefits are offered with many full-time jobs. Full medical benefits generally include medical insurance, dental insurance, and vision care. On jobs with benefits, workers may also get medical care for their husband or wife and children. In general, part-time workers get limited benefits or no benefits at all. Check with your employer to find out which medical benefits are offered with your job.

**B** May Ling went to the doctor in December with a bad cough and chest pain. The doctor took blood and urine tests. The test results showed pneumonia. May went back and was given antibiotics and told to rest at home and drink lots of fluids. In January, May returned to be rechecked by the doctor.

Work with your classmates and read the benefits statement.

## Statement of Medical Benefits

| **Dates of Service** | **Company Name** | **Claim Number** |
|---|---|---|
| 12/8/97–1/5/98 | IGT Corporation | 921-31-6720 |

| **Patient's Name** | **Group Number** | **ID #** |
|---|---|---|
| May Ling | 92371 | 456-12-6524 |

| Service Date | Type of Service | Total Billed | Not Allowed | Deductible | Insurance Payment |
|---|---|---|---|---|---|
| 12/8/97 | Medical visit | 50.00 | 0.00 | 15.00 | 35.00 |
| 12/8/97 | Lab fees | 75.00 | 7.50 | | 67.50 |
| 12/8/97 | X-Ray | 45.00 | | | 45.00 |
| 12/13/97 | Medical visit | 50.00 | | 15.00 | 35.00 |
| 12/15/97 | Prescription | 42.00 | | 5.00 | 37.00 |
| 1/5/98 | Medical visit | 50.00 | | 15.00 | 35.00 |
| 1/5/98 | Lab fees | 35.00 | 3.50 | | 31.50 |
| **Total** | | **347.00** | **11.00** | **50.00** | **286.00** |

For further information call: (212) 555-8211

**C** Answer these questions about the statement of benefits and the information.

1. How many times did May Ling visit the doctor in December and January? _____

2. What three other charges (not medical visits) show up on the statement?

   _____  _____  _____

3. What was the total billed for lab fees (blood and urine tests)? _____

4. After all deductions and allowances, how much did the insurance company pay for lab fees? _____

5. How much did the insurance company pay for May Ling's pneumonia treatment? _____

★ 6. What could May Ling have done to prevent this illness?

   _____

★ 7. Why do you think medical treatment is so expensive?

   _____

★ **D** If you can, bring in copies of statements of medical benefits. Explain the information in the statements to members of a group. Who can you call if you have questions about the information in the benefits' statement?

★ **E** Discuss these questions with your teammates. What can a worker do if she or he does not have medical insurance? Is it possible to get your own private medical insurance? Are the costs of private medical insurance low or high? Why? What determines the rates of medical insurance? What information do medical insurance companies want to see before they give insurance to workers?

## 10. Listening at Work: Benefits

**A** As you listen to the conversation, take notes on the benefits and the dates.

**1.** Benefit _____

   Dates _____

**2.** Benefit _____

   Dates _____

**3.** Benefit _____

   Dates _____

**4.** Benefit _____

   Dates _____

**B** Listen to the conversation again. With a partner, make up an additional conversation about benefits and act it out in front of the class.

## 11. Workplace Vocabulary

| seniority | labor union | grievance |
| contract | strike | Civil Rights Act |
| medical insurance | handicapped | benefits |

**A** Fill in the following sentences using the workplace vocabulary words. Compare your answers with your classmates. Then find the pages where the words are used in this chapter and fill in the page numbers. Compare the sentences you found in the chapter with the sentences on this page.

**Page Number**

1. A _____ _____ is an organization _____ that represents workers.

2. Workers hired after Ali were laid off first _____ because Ali had _____.

3. After the members of a union vote to stop _____ working, they go on _____.

4. A written complaint against an employer is a _____ _____.

5. The _____ _____ _____ _____ of 1964 says there will be no discrimination based on race.

6. Alitash works full time at the hospital. She gets _____ _____ _____ as a benefit.

7. A union _____ guarantees job _____ protection and benefits.

8. Goi can't hear. She is _____. _____

9. Medical insurance, retirement pay, paid holidays, _____ and sick pay are _____.

**B** Select two vocabulary words from the list. Write each word on a piece of paper. Ask another student to give a definition of your word and to use the word in a sentence. When you finish with one student, move to another and repeat the definition and sentence work.

## 12. Assessing Your Progress

**A** Answer the following questions.

1. What are four things guaranteed in a union contract?

   _____      _____

   _____      _____

2. From what you learned in this chapter about unions, what are some of the advantages of being a union member? What are some of the disadvantages?

   _____      _____

   _____      _____

3. What federal laws protect working people from discrimination?

by age: _____

by sex: _____

by disability: _____

by race, color, religion, sex, and nationality: _____

_____

for organizing a union: _____

4. What is considered full-time work (how many hours)?

_____

5. What is considered part-time work (how many hours)?

_____

6. Would you prefer to work full time or part time? Why?

_____

7. What information can you find in a medical statement of benefits?

_____

_____

_____

# 13. Looking Back

| **A** Things I learned about about unions, labor laws, and benefits | How I can apply what I learned to my life |
|---|---|
| 1. | |
| 2. | |
| 3. | |
| **B** New words and idioms | Related words from my job |
| 1. | |
| 2. | |
| 3. | |

## CHAPTER 1: DESCRIBING WITH ADJECTIVES

**A** Read the paragraph and answer the questions.

A woman with many years of experience in building construction saw a construction job advertised in the newspaper. She called to talk to the foreman. The foreman asked her, "Do you really think a woman can do this kind of work? This is men's work." She told him, "Of course I can. I have ten years experience doing construction." They made an appointment. When she arrived at the interview a sign was posted on the door. It said, "All jobs filled, no more interviews."

1. Describe the type of personality you think the woman had.
2. What type of personality do you think the foreman had?
3. What do you think the woman did after she read the sign?
★ 4. What personal qualities are necessary to be "A woman in a man's world" or "A man in a woman's world"?

**B** Think about a coworker or a friend's personality. Look at the list of qualities below. Which qualities describe the person you know?

| | | | |
|---|---|---|---|
| talkative | neat and clean | patient | crazy |
| quiet | easygoing | aggressive | selfish |
| serious | hardworking | cowardly | dependable |
| funny | competitive | persistent | lazy |
| outgoing | angry | courageous | friendly |
| practical | honest | shy | untrustworthy |
| uptight | stubborn | impolite | trustworthy |

**Examples:** *My friend is _____ because _____.*
*My coworker is _____, but she isn't _____.*

**C** Select the qualities from the list above that will be helpful when looking for a job.

*Example: Be persistent!*

_____

_____

_____

_____

_____

**A** Read the story.

**How I Got My Job** by Yoshi Ozaki

I used to be an English teacher in a kindergarten in Japan. While working there I always wondered if it was the right job for me. I enjoyed teaching, but sometimes I didn't feel completely satisfied.

One day I went to an employment agency. They were looking for tour conductors who could speak English. I thought, "This is it! I've finally found the job I've been looking for." Then I went to the job interview. I told them how much I was interested in the tour conductor job. I was very eager.

One week later I got the job. It was fun and interesting. I went to other countries and met other people. It was a great opportunity for me. I really enjoyed working as a tour conductor.

**B** Write six questions about the story. Begin your questions with the question words *Who, What, Where, When, Why, How,* and *How long.*

*Example:* What was her job before she was a tour conductor?

1. _____

2. _____

3. _____

4. _____

5. _____

6. _____

Ask another student to check your questions.

**C** Walk around the classroom. Ask three classmates your questions about the story.

**A** Look at the pictures. Read the information. Each person is applying for an office manager job in an extremely busy book publishing company.

**1**
**Name:** Mona Naser
**Age:** 60
**Born:** Egypt
**Moved to U.S.:** 1962
**Work Experience:** Secretary in legal office for ten years in U.S., fluent in English. Has a lot of experience with computers.
**Personality:** Likes to work independently, hardworking, trouble getting along with others

**2**
**Name:** Wu Xiang Hua
**Age:** 30
**Born:** People's Republic of China
**Moved to U.S.:** 1990
**Work Experience:** Assistant office manager for publisher for five years in U.S. Still has some problems speaking English. Excellent computer skills.
**Personality:** Good team skills

**3**
**Name:** Reyna Alvarez
**Age:** 25
**Born:** United States
**Moved to U.S.:** Native born
**Work Experience:** Two years working as an office receptionist. Difficulty using correct grammar.
**Personality:** Competitive and serious

**4**
**Name:** Anthony Sawitsky
**Age:** 21
**Born:** United States
**Moved to U.S.:** Native born
**Work Experience:** None. Getting a Bachelor's Degree in Business Administration. Excellent writing skills.
**Personality:** Well organized and willing to work overtime

**B** Make a check (✔) under the job experience of each person. Then, review the information with a partner.

*Example:* **a.** *Has Mona had experience in the book publishing business?*
**b.** *Yes, she's had five years experience.*

| | 1 | 2 | 3 | 4 |
|---|---|---|---|---|
| experience publishing books | | | | |
| experience running an office | | | | |
| experience working with people with different kinds of personalities | | | | |
| experience using English on the job | | | | |
| experience using computers | | | | |
| experience managing an office | | | | |

**C** Compare the job applicants.

*Example:* *Reyna Alvarez has had two years experience working in an office, but Anthony Sawitsky has had no experience.*

Decide which person you would hire for the job. Give reasons why.

*Example:* I would hire _____ because he or she _____.

# CHAPTER 4: ASKING FOR CLARIFICATION

**A** Use Clarification Questions to confirm information or instructions. Use *Do you mean, Do you want me to,* or *Did you say* to begin your questions.

1. When you leave work, don't forget to turn off your computer and take the mail to the post office.

    *Do you mean to turn off the machine first, and then go to the post office?*

2. When the temperature is over 75 degrees, please turn on the air conditioning.

    _____

    _____

3. First, I want you to drain the oil. Then, check the spark plugs.

    _____

    _____

4. First, fill the sink with soapy water. Then, put the dishes in the sink. Wash the dishes and dry them.

    _____

    _____

5. Please answer the telephones and take messages for everyone in the office.

    _____

    _____

6. Work with reading group A for 30 minutes and then take them to the cafeteria.

    _____

    _____

**B** Write about a situation in which a supervisor is giving instructions to a worker. Then, ask your partner to write a question confirming the instructions.

_____

_____

_____

_____

# CHAPTER 5: TALKING ABOUT THE PAST

**A** Think of some work you or someone else did in the past. Answer the questions using past tense verbs.

**1.** What was the job?

_____

_____

**2.** How did you find that job?

_____

_____

**3.** What skills did you need for that job?

_____

_____

**4.** What responsibilities did you have?

_____

_____

**5.** Did you get along with your coworkers and supervisor?

_____

_____

**6.** What did you like about that job? What didn't you like about that job?

_____

_____

**7.** How long did you work on that job?

_____

_____

**8.** Why did you leave that job?

_____

_____

**B** Now, interview a partner about his or her past work experience.

**C** When you go to a job interview, you want to sound assertive and confident. Record your interview or practice it in front of a group.

**A** Read the supervisor's evaluation.

| | YEVGENY | SAUL | FATIMA | BORIS |
|---|---|---|---|---|
| **Responsible**<br>completes all work<br>on time | ✔ | ✔ | ✔ | ✔ |
| **Friendly**<br>gets along well<br>with coworkers | ✔ | ✔ | ✔ | ✔ |
| **Conscientious**<br>serious about doing<br>his or her work | ✔ | | | ✔ |
| **Active Team Member**<br>works well in a group,<br>suggests new ideas | ✔ | ✔ | | ✔ |
| **Neat and well organized**<br>keeps work area clean,<br>materials are easy to find | | | ✔ | ✔ |
| **Leader**<br>motivates others to do<br>the necessary work,<br>sets a good example | | | | ✔ |

**B** Summarize the information above. Work with a partner. Compare your sentences.

**Example:** *All of the employees are responsible and friendly.*

_____

_____

_____

_____

_____

**C** Now, use the personal qualities in Section A to evaluate your coworkers or someone you know.

_____

_____

_____

_____

**A** It is Friday afternoon at 5:00 P.M. Monisha has just received her paycheck for last week. She has changed departments and her pay should be higher now. If the information is not correct, she will have to ask the payroll department to correct the check.

| EMPLOYEE NAME | MONISHA PATEL | | | | DESCRIPTION | TAXES/DED. | TOTAL GROSS PAY | TOTAL NET PAY |
|---|---|---|---|---|---|---|---|---|
| EMPLOYEE NUMBER | 65902 | | | | FEDERAL TAX | 20.00 | | |
| PAY PERIOD | 12/13/97–12/19/97 | | | | STATE TAX | .20 | | |
| AMOUNT OF CHECK | 339.65 | | | | FICA | 23.90 | | |
| | HOURS | PAY RATE | THIS PERIOD | | MEDICARE | 6.25 | | |
| | | | | | MEDICAL INSURANCE | 30.00 | | |
| REGULAR | 40 | 8.00 | 320.00 | | UNION DUES | 20.00 | | |
| OVERTIME | 10 | 12.00 | 120.00 | | | | | |
| YEAR-TO-DATE REGULAR | | | 19350.00 | | YEAR-TO-DATE GROSS | 22150.00 | | |
| YEAR-TO-DATE OVERTIME | | | 2800.00 | | YEAR-TO-DATE NET | 18610.00 | 440.00 | 339.65 |

**B** You are Monisha's coworker. Help her review her pay stub.

1. a. *Would you check the pay period? It was December 13–December 19, 1997.*

   b. *Yes, it's correct.* _____

2. a. _____ check the hours? There should be 40 hours at regular time and 14 hours at overtime.

   b. _____

3. a. _____ the pay? The regular pay should be $10.00 an hour and overtime should be $15.00 an hour.

   b. _____

4. How many different problems did Monisha find in her paycheck?

**C** What would you suggest Monisha say to the bookkeeper in payroll about her pay stub?

*Would you check* _____

*It should show* _____

_____

**D** What parts of her paycheck did Monisha learn she needs to review every week?

_____

_____

▲ Gabriel Zayas

**A** Read the story.

**Karate** by Gabriel Zayas

When I was a teenager living in Mexico City, my friends and I used to go to the movies to watch Bruce Lee performing martial arts. At that time I was about 13-years old. From the first time I saw Bruce Lee on the screen, I knew that I liked martial arts. It was beautiful! After I began high school, from the age of 15-to-17, I practiced martial arts every day. I liked the discipline of martial arts and the control it gave me over my body.

When I was 19, I received my black belt. My parents were very excited and proud of me. I started my own school in Mexico City when I was 20. There were adults and children in my classes, between the ages of 5 and 30. There were between 30 and 50 students in each class.

I started my school in the United States in 1991, six years after I arrived in this country. My school is called the International Tumanao Institute. We teach a Polynesian style of Karate called Limalama. Limalama means wisdom. This style of karate is for self defense and recreation. We teach our students self respect and discipline. Our style of Karate is not for combat or fighting.

**B** Write four questions about Gabriel's story. Begin your questions with the words, *"How long has Gabriel . . . ?"* or *"How long did Gabriel . . . ?"*

*Example: How long has Gabriel been living in the United States?*

1. _____

2. _____

3. _____

4. _____

**C** Walk around the classroom. Ask three classmates your questions about the story.

**D** Tell a classmate your life story. Answer questions your classmate asks about your story.

# Application For Employment
## An Equal Opportunity Employer

## PERSONAL INFORMATION

NAME

SOCIAL SECURITY NUMBER

Last                    First                    Middle

HOME ADDRESS

STREET

TELEPHONE NUMBER

CITY                    STATE                    ZIP CODE

POSITION DESIRED            SALARY EXPECTED            FULL TIME
                                                       PART TIME
DATE YOU CAN START _____            TEMPORARY

## GENERAL INFORMATION

| | | |
|---|---|---|
| DO YOU HAVE THE LEGAL RIGHT TO REMAIN AND WORK IN THE UNITED STATES? | YES ☐ | NO ☐ |
| HAVE YOU EVER BEEN CONVICTED OF A FELONY? If yes, explain: | YES ☐ | NO ☐ |
| ARE YOU OVER THE AGE OF 18? | YES ☐ | NO ☐ |
| HAVE YOU EVER WORKED FOR THIS COMPANY BEFORE? If so, when? _____ | YES ☐ | NO ☐ |
| DO YOU HAVE A VALID DRIVER'S LICENSE? | YES ☐ | NO ☐ |
| HAS YOUR DRIVER'S LICENSE EVER BEEN SUSPENDED OR REVOKED? | YES ☐ | NO ☐ |

## EDUCATIONAL INFORMATION

| NAME OF SCHOOL | ADDRESS | FROM/TO | MAJOR SUBJECT | DEGREE? Yes/No |
|---|---|---|---|---|
| High School | | | | |
| Vocational or Training School | | | | |
| College or University | | | | |
| Graduate School | | | | |

# WORK EXPERIENCE

| COMPANY NAME | PHONE NUMBER |
|---|---|
| ADDRESS | EMPLOYMENT DATES<br>FROM          TO |
| POSITION HELD | SALARY |
| DUTIES AND RESPONSIBILITIES | |
| SUPERVISOR'S NAME | REASON FOR LEAVING |

| COMPANY NAME | PHONE NUMBER |
|---|---|
| ADDRESS | EMPLOYMENT DATES<br>FROM          TO |
| POSITION HELD | SALARY |
| DUTIES AND RESPONSIBILITIES | |
| SUPERVISOR'S NAME | REASON FOR LEAVING |

| COMPANY NAME | PHONE NUMBER |
|---|---|
| ADDRESS | EMPLOYMENT DATES<br>FROM          TO |
| POSITION HELD | SALARY |
| DUTIES AND RESPONSIBILITIES | |
| SUPERVISOR'S NAME | REASON FOR LEAVING |

| CAN YOU OPERATE A PERSONAL COMPUTER? | WHICH MODEL/PROGRAMS? |
|---|---|

WHAT OTHER MACHINES CAN YOU OPERATE?

ARE YOU FLUENT IN ANY LANGUAGES OTHER THAN ENGLISH?

MAY WE CONTACT YOUR LAST EMPLOYER FOR A REFERENCE?          YES          NO

## REFERENCES

| NAME | RELATIONSHIP | PHONE NUMBER | YEARS KNOWN |
|---|---|---|---|
| | | | |
| | | | |

I certify that the information in this application is true and correct to the best of my knowledge. I authorize any of the persons or organizations referenced in this application to give you any and all information concerning my previous employment, education, or any other information that might have with regard to the subjects in this application. I release all parties from all liability for damages. I authorize you to request and receive such information. I understand that all offers of employment are conditioned on being able to supply satisfactory proof of an applicant's identity and legal authority to work in the United States.

Date _____          Signature of Applicant _____

## ▶ Chapter 1: Looking for and Finding a Job

### 7. D. Job Interview Questions and Answers

*Narrator:* Listen to the questions and circle the correct responses.

1. *Speaker 1:* What position are you applying for?
   *Speaker 2:*
   a. The Personnel Office is on your right.
   b. Auto body repair person.
   c. I did maintenance work in my country.

2. *Speaker 1:* What did you do on your last job?
   *Speaker 3:*
   a. I was employed as a dental hygienist.
   b. Gardening is my hobby.
   c. My sister worked in the main office.

3. *Speaker 1:* How much experience do you have?
   *Speaker 4:*
   a. I worked as a carpenter for seven years.
   b. I moved to the United States five years ago.
   c. I want to be a computer operator.

4. *Speaker 1:* Please describe yourself.
   *Speaker 5:*
   a. I have two children.
   b. Third shift is best for me.
   c. I'm hardworking and honest.

5. *Speaker 1:* What skills do you have?
   *Speaker 6:*
   a. I can cook and clean, and I'm good at taking care of children.
   b. I have a car.
   c. I can work any shift.

6. *Speaker 1:* What days and hours would you prefer to work?
   *Speaker 7:*
   a. I can operate a computer.
   b. I would prefer to work day shift during the week.
   c. My children are in school.

### 10. A. What We Say at Work

*Narrator:* Listen to the job interviews. Circle if the applicant's answer is Yes or No.

1. *Speaker 1:* Do you have the legal right to work in this country?
   *Speaker 2:* Here is my work permit.

2. *Speaker 1:* Are you over the age of 18?
   *Speaker 2:* I turned 18 last year.

3. *Speaker 1:* Are you working now?
   *Speaker 2:* I work at Food 4 You. I'm a stock clerk.

4. *Speaker 1:* Can we contact your present employer?
   *Speaker 2:* I'd rather you didn't contact him. He doesn't know I'm looking for a job.

5. *Speaker 1:* Has anyone in your family worked for this company before?
   *Speaker 2:* My sister worked here five years ago.

## ▶ Chapter 2: Starting a New Job

### 8. A. Work Memos

*Narrator:* Companies often call meetings for new employees. Listen to two new workers discussing a work memo. Then answer the questions.

*Speaker 1:*
Memo to: New employees on the first shift
From:     Jean Nagano,
            Personnel Director
Date:      September 20, 1998
**Orientation meeting**
**Attendance is mandatory.**

*Speaker 1:* On Friday, September 25, from 10:00 to 11:00 A.M. our company will hold an orientation meeting for all new first-shift employees in the lunchroom. Attendance is mandatory. Information about work rules and safety will be discussed. Refreshments will be served.
*Speaker 2:* Did you hear about that orientation meeting?
*Speaker 3:* Yeah, when is it?
*Speaker 2:* It's on the 25 at 10 A.M.

**Speaker 3:** What's it for?

**Speaker 2:** Orientation. You know—when they talk to you about rules and safety.

**Speaker 3:** Do we have to go?

**Speaker 2:** Yes. It's mandatory. You have to go.

**Speaker 3:** Okay. Where is it?

**Speaker 2:** In the lunchroom. And they're going to serve food!

**Narrator:** Now answer the questions about the memo.

## 10. A. First Day of Work Issues

**Narrator:** Listen to these questions about work. What specific information is given? Circle the appropriate answer.

1. **Worker 1:** Where do we punch in and out?

   **Supervisor 1:** The first thing you do when you come in is punch in at the time clock. You punch in and out at the clock in front of the supervisor's office.

   **Worker 1:** Where do we punch in and out?

   **Narrator:** a. near the Personnel Office
   b. near the supervisor's office

2. **Worker 2:** What clothing am I required to wear on the job?

   **Supervisor 2:** You'll need to wear long pants, a long-sleeved shirt, goggles for your eyes, and leather work shoes every day. This safety clothing will protect you from any flying pieces of metal.

   **Worker 2:** What clothing am I required to wear on the job?

   **Narrator:** a. long pants, a long-sleeved shirt, goggles, and leather shoes
   b. long pants and a T-shirt

3. **Worker 3:** Where can I buy safety shoes?

   **Supervisor 3:** You'll need leather shoes. Don't wear sandals or anything with an open toe. Go to Black Hawk Shoes. It's a work shoe place on Fifth near Broadway.

   **Worker 3:** Where can I buy safety shoes?

   **Narrator:** a. Black Tree Shoes
   b. Black Hawk Shoes

4. **Worker 4:** When can I take a break?

   **Supervisor 4:** It's from 10:00 to 10:15 A.M. Be back at your work station at 10:15. Don't be late!

   **Worker 4:** When can I take a break?

**Narrator:** a. 10:00 A.M.–10:30 A.M.
b. 10:00 A.M.–10:15 A.M.

5. **Worker 5:** Where is the restroom?

   **Supervisor 5:** There are two restrooms in the building. One is on the first floor and the other is on the second floor. The one on this floor is in room 126. It's down the hall on your right, just past the cafeteria.

   **Worker 5:** Where is the restroom?

   **Narrator:** a. near the cafeteria
   b. near the tool crib

## ▶ Chapter 3: Technology and Training

## 6. A. Listening at Work

**Narrator:** A supervisor is giving information about training classes to his employees. Listen to the information and fill in the schedule.

**Supervisor:** As you know, this electronics factory will be closing on June 15th of next year. We've been in business for 50 years now, but this past year we have lost too much business to the competition. We're giving each of you the opportunity to develop other skills that will help you find a new job. The company will pay for your training classes.

The Basic Math and Reading classes will begin September 19 at 1:00 P.M., at the end of the shift. They will be two-hour classes, five days a week, in room 107.

For those on the second shift, Basic Math and Reading will start on October 1 and will go from 9:00 P.M. to 11:00 P.M. Class will be in the back of the cafeteria. In the math and reading classes you'll refresh your memory on reading skills and math skills: addition, subtraction, division, and multiplication.

ESL, English as a Second Language, classes will start here on October 13 if you need more practice in speaking, reading, or writing in English after the first shift.

Technical training classes in Air Conditioning and Heating Repair and Machine Shop begin in January, just after New Year's. January 5th for Air Conditioning and Heating. Machine Shop starts January 20. Both are at 1:00 P.M. at Main Street School.

If you want to get a high school diploma, GED Preparation classes will be offered at Central High School, Monday through Friday from 3:00 P.M. to 6:00 P.M., beginning immediately.

Oh yes, a special class in Auto Body Repair has been added. It will be offered at night, from 6:00 to 10:00 P.M. at Sammy's Auto Repair. It begins September 30.

We hope that each of you will decide to attend these free classes. You can take as many as you want. Sign up for them in the office with the Personnel Director, Mr. Burns, before September 15.

## 8. D. Understanding the Workplace

*Narrator:* Work in groups of four. Imagine you are career advisors. Listen to each speaker. Discuss what each speaker can do. Listen to each situation again. Choose one situation to act out.

Advances in technology may affect every job in the future. What should each worker do?

1. *Margarita:* I'm Margarita. I have two kids. They're 5 and 9. My husband works from 2 to 11 every day. I work at General Telephone from 9 A.M. to 5 P.M. I'm one of the supervisors of Directory Assistance. Can you believe it? Last week I got a notice that the company was eliminating my job. They said, take a layoff (no job!) or transfer to another department. Now, if I transfer, I have to take a training class after work. They'll pay for the class, but not for my time. And besides that, who will take care of my kids in the evening?
   *Narrator:* What should Margarita do?
   a. Look for a new job
   b. Take the training class and pay a babysitter
   c. Bring her children to the class with her
   d. Get information about programs that might help her change jobs

2. *David:* Let me introduce myself. My name is David. After I finished high school I studied to be an electrician at a technical school. Then I worked at an aircraft company for six years. When there were no more airplanes to make, they laid me off. I had no work for six months! Finally, two weeks ago, I got an electrical job at a machine shop. But everything is different there. It's all computerized. I don't understand how to use their computers! It's very confusing. If I make a lot of mistakes, I'll lose this job.
   *Narrator:* What can David do?
   a. Ask other workers on the job for help
   b. Ask the supervisor for additional help
   c. Stay on the job while getting more training at school
   d. Ask to observe another worker before or after his regular hours

3. *Tatiana:* I'm Tatiana. I don't like to talk about it, but I'm 55 years old. I work in the word processing department at Annuity Insurance Company. The pay is about $10.00 per hour plus benefits. I've worked there for about five years. Yesterday I heard a rumor that 50 percent of the people in my department are going to be laid off. They just don't need us anymore. I 'm too old to go look for another job!
   *Narrator:* What can Tatiana do?
   a. Say nothing and wait for more information
   b. Ask the supervisor if the rumors are true
   c. Ask other workers about the rumors
   d. Find out about job placement programs for older workers

4. *Chen:* My name is Chen. When I lived in China I carved beautiful vases and crystal in a glass factory. I had a lot of experience, almost 20 years. After I came to the United States, I thought I could find the same job here. But to work in a glass factory here you need to know good English and how to use computer programs. I know English, but just a little . . . and I have to support my family!
   *Narrator:* What can Chen do?
   a. Look for another job and hope his English improves
   b. Study English as a Second Language at school
   c. Study ESL at home on television
   d. Ask his children to translate for him

## ▶ Chapter 4: Communicating with Your Boss

### 5. D. Receiving, Repeating, and Checking Information

*Narrator:* Listen to the conversations. Circle who you think is speaking.

1. *Narrator:* Who do you think is speaking?
   *Speaker 1:* When you finish painting the bedrooms, do the living room. Use the off-white in the bedrooms and the light beige in the living room. Remember, don't drip any paint on the floors.
   *Narrator:* Who do you think is speaking?
   a. contractor    b. painter

2. *Narrator:* Who do you think is speaking?
   *Speaker 2:* Mr. Tuttle in room 5 needs a doctor. Can you call a doctor? When I went in his room he was having bad pains in his back and he asked me to tell you. I wanted to help, but I think he needs some medication from a doctor.
   *Narrator:* Who do you think is speaking?
   a. nurse    b. nursing assistant

3. *Narrator:* Who do you think is speaking?
   *Speaker 3:* Diem, you did a great job yesterday. You delivered all the newspapers on your route to all the correct addresses. Keep up the good work!
   *Narrator:* Who do you think is speaking?
   a. supervisor
   b. newspaper delivery person

4. *Narrator:* Who do you think is speaking?
   *Speaker 4:* Hi Mrs. Smedley. This is Qi. Can you please buy some Quick Clean for the windows and some oven cleaner? We're all out. Thanks. I really appreciate you doing this for me.
   *Narrator:* Who do you think is speaking?
   a. housekeeper    b. homemaker

5. *Narrator:* Who do you think is speaking?
   *Speaker 5:* Hello Amy. Today you will be working in three different departments. That's part of your training. First you'll help Tom put out the bread and cakes in the bakery department. Then, you'll be pricing the cheese and stocking the deli department. After lunch you will be working on the cash register.

*Narrator:* Who do you think is speaking?
   a. store manager
   b. supermarket stocker

*Narrator:* Listen to the conversations again. What was each person asked to do?

1. a. paint the bathroom
   b. paint the living room
2. a. contact a doctor
   b. call the police
3. a. quit
   b. continue to do the same good work
4. a. buy window cleaner
   b. buy paper towels
5. a. continue to do the same good work
   b. be flexible

### 10. A. What We Say at Work

*Narrator:* Listen to the conversation. Put a check next to the items you hear about in the talk.

*Mrs. Perry:* A warm welcome to all of you new employees at Ampex Corporation. And congratulations to you on becoming a part of such a wonderful company. I'm Mrs. Perry and I will be your supervisor in the Word Processing Department.

Now, as for supplies, if you need a stapler, paper, or pencils please ask me. I can order them for you. If your computer needs to be fixed, call the Repair Department; they will be up here in a jiffy. But you really shouldn't need them because the machines are almost new. If the copier or the fax machine is not working and needs to be repaired, call those wonderful repairpeople. And, by the way everyone, we don't waste paper here, we recycle it. As you know, we're saving those trees.

Now, what else do I need to tell you? Oh yes, about the time records. You are expected to turn your time sheets in to me on Fridays before you go home at five. Don't forget to write down your working hours each day.

If you will be drinking coffee and want to join our coffee club, talk to May Chan. May, wave your hand. There she is. She's our coffee club, birthday party, and holiday party organizer. We try to celebrate everyone's birthday together because we're such a happy family. As you already know, the restrooms are down the hall from the main office. And by the way, don't forget to let me know before you go out for lunch every day. That way I can keep track of your time away from your machines.

I look forward to having all of you in our department.

## 10. B. What We Say at Work

*Narrator:* Listen to the conversation again and write the names of the people or departments you are supposed to contact. Use **S** for supervisor, **R** for repair department, and **P** for the party organizer.

## ▶ Chapter 5: Work in My Home Country, Work in My New Country

## 7. C. Career and Changes

*Narrator:* Listen to each worker's story. Listen for the reason why each moved from one country to another. Circle the correct answers.

1. *Speaker 1:* Teresa was born in El Salvador. For many years she worked as an elementary school teacher in a small town. Some of the teachers in her school were killed in the civil war. The government closed her school. She couldn't find another job, so she decided to move to the United States.
   *Narrator:* Why did she come to the United States?
   **a.** religious reasons     **b.** political reasons

2. *Speaker 2:* Alicia Oh was born in the United States. When she was 15 years old her parents returned to their native country of South Korea. Her parents wanted to live closer to other members of their family. Alicia was never happy after she returned to South Korea. The culture was too different from the United States. When she was 23 she moved back to the United States.
   *Narrator:* Why did her parents return to Korea?
   **a.** war     **b.** family reasons

3. *Speaker 3:* Saad came from a family of 10 children. They lived on a farm in Yemen.

He was the oldest son. He moved to the United States to help support his family.
*Narrator:* Why did he move to the United States?
**a.** religious reasons
**b.** economic reasons

4. *Speaker 4:* During the war in Vietnam Thu Nguyen escaped from her country in a small fishing boat. She traveled for seven days on the water with many other men, women, and children. Finally, the boat landed in the United States.
   *Narrator:* Why did she come to the United States?
   **a.** religious reasons     **b.** war

## 9. B. What We Say at Work

*Narrator:* Listen to these job interviews. What does each worker say about his or her reason for leaving the last job? Circle the appropriate answer.

1. *Interviewer 1:* Why did you leave your last job?
   *Huong:* I left my job when I came to the United States. My father was already living here and he told me to move here.
   *Narrator:* Why did she leave her last job?
   **a.** She moved to a new country.
   **b.** She was laid off.

2. *Interviewer 2:* What was your reason for leaving your last job?
   *Arturo:* My leg was broken on my last job in an accident. Some boxes fell on it. I went on a medical leave. After the accident I decided to look for a new job.
   *Narrator:* Why did he leave his last job?
   **a.** He was fired.
   **b.** He had a work accident.

3. *Interviewer 1:* Why did you stop working for the insurance company? You had a good job.
   *Naomi:* I liked the job, but it was boring. I wanted a job that was more of a challenge. This job uses more of my computer and math skills.
   *Narrator:* Why did she leave her last job?
   **a.** Because she had a work accident.
   **b.** Because she wanted a better job.

**4. Interviewer 2:** Why did you leave your last job?

**Sara:** My father was sick and I was the only person to take care of him.

**Interviewer 2:** Are you still taking care of him?

**Sara:** No, he is better now.

**Narrator:** Why did she leave her last job?

a. Because she had family problems.

b. Because she didn't like the job.

**5. Interviewer 1:** Why did you stop working at the factory?

**Hillel:** The factory shut down. There wasn't any more work. The supervisor said he'd call me when there was more work.

**Interviewer 1:** Did you quit your job?

**Hillel:** No, I was laid off.

**Narrator:** Why did he leave his last job?

a. He was fired.     b. He was laid off.

**6. Interviewer 2:** Why were you late so often for your last job?

**Marina:** My youngest son had problems with gangs on his way to school. I had to walk him to school every day to protect him.

**Interviewer 2:** Are you going to continue to be late for work?

**Marina:** No, he transferred to another school.

**Narrator:** Why did she leave her last job?

a. Because she had a personal injury.

b. Because she had family problems.

▶ **Chapter 6: Work Schedules and Paychecks**

## 6. A. Situations-Company Policies and Schedules

*Narrator:* Sit in a small group. Listen to and read the scenes below. What should each worker do?

**1. Speaker 1:** You are an emergency room orderly at County Hospital working the day shift. The orderly on the next shift calls in sick with the flu. Your supervisor asks you to work a second shift. You would receive time-and-a-half pay for every extra hour you work. Your problem is you are supposed to take your children to see their favorite Uncle Joe, who is visiting from out of town. Uncle Joe only comes to visit once every two years. He's 78 and you don't know when you will see him again.

*Narrator:* What should you do? Should you work overtime? Explain.

**2. Speaker 2:** You are a father with three children and a lot of bills. You work the day shift at a car wash six days a week. Last week you worked as a night security guard to make extra money. Every day for the last week you got to work late because you overslept. Your boss has told you that the next time you come to work late you'll be fired.

*Narrator:* What should you do? Should you continue to work the two jobs? Why?

**3. Speaker 3:** Rosa is a postal carrier with three school-aged children. She has an urgent appointment to speak with her childrens' teachers at 6 P.M. At 4 P.M. she finishes delivering the mail. Her supervisor asks her if she can work an extra three hours and deliver the mail on another carrier's route.

*Narrator:* What should Rosa do? Should she see her childrens' teachers or work the overtime?

**4. Speaker 4:** Bob teaches English as a Second Language to adults. He works every morning, Monday to Friday, from 8:30 A.M. to 12:30 P.M. His wife is sick with cancer. When he comes to work he has trouble concentrating and frequently yells at his students. His supervisor meets with Bob and explains that Bob can't bring his personal problems to work.

*Narrator:* What should Bob do? How can he concentrate on his work?

## 9. E. Situations—Paychecks, Pay Stubs, and Deductions

*Narrator:* Listen to the conversation. Write the kind of deduction on the line.

**1. Speaker 1:** I had my baby last year! Isn't she cute? She's just getting some teeth. Without that medical insurance from work, I don't know what I'd have done. It paid for the birth and the well baby visits and all the prescriptions. Oh. Ok honey. Are you hungry? Mommy has some food for you.

*Narrator:* What is the deduction?

2. *Speaker 2:* It's money the government pays back to you when you're 65. It's not a lot. Doesn't cover all my expenses. We used to think you could retire on it, but not anymore. At least it will pay some of my bills after I retire. And I've been paying into it all my working life.

*Narrator:* What is the deduction?

3. *Speaker 3:* Every month they take that money out of my check. It pays for the union building and contract negotiations and all the papers they send out to us and all. It helps the union represent me and that's really important.

*Narrator:* What is the deduction?

4. *Speaker 4:* The federal government, they take all that money out every month. It pays for Congress and schools and roads and wars. I know it's important to run the government. I'm glad they at least take it out of every check and not just once at the end of the year.

*Narrator:* What is the deduction?

## ▶ Chapter 7: Safety

## 7. A. Understanding the Workplace

*Narrator:* Work in a group. Imagine that you work in the shipping department of an appliance manufacturing company. There is a problem with the ventilation system. Listen to the conversation. With your teammates, discuss the questions.

*Victor:* Mr. Schilling? I'm Victor from the Shipping Department. We need your help.

*Mr. Schilling:* Yes, Victor. What can I do for you?

*Victor:* There's no heat in our department. This is the third day there's been no heat.

*Mr. Schilling:* I had someone in maintenance check the ventilation yesterday. They told me there was no problem. But it is awfully cold here.

*Victor:* Could you have the maintenance supervisor check the ventilation again? We can't do our work because it's too cold.

*Mr. Schilling:* Okay. But don't stop working!

*Narrator:*

What problem is Victor reporting?

Does Mr. Schilling think there is a heating problem?

What did Victor request that Mr. Schilling do about the problem?

What was Mr. Shilling's response?

What do you think will happen?

## 7. C. Understanding the Workplace

*Narrator:* Work in a group of four. Listen to each speaker. Then discuss what each individual or group can do. Act out each situation in your group or in front of your class.

1. *Speaker 1:* In the winter it's always cold in this department. In the summer it's very hot, over 100 degrees. It's difficult to breathe. There is no cross-ventilation. We've asked the supervisor for a fan and a heater. After we talk to the supervisor, nothing ever happens. What can we do?

*Narrator:* What can they do?

a. Smile and keep working. Be happy to have a job.

b. Buy their own heaters and fans.

c. Write a memo to the safety committee. Then meet with the committee to discuss the problem.

d. Refuse to work until the ventilator is repaired.

2. *Speaker 2:* I work in an electronics factory on the night shift. All night long I inspect circuit boards to make sure they are wired correctly. The problem is the lights. Last week some of the lights above my work space went out. It was almost impossible to see the boards. We couldn't see if the work was correct or not. The manager said he would fix the lights, but he hasn't fixed them yet.

*Narrator:* What can the speaker do?

a. Bring in his own lamp.

b. Check with the manager. Get a definite date when the lights will be replaced.

c. Call in sick every day until the lights are replaced.

d. Ask to move to another space.

3. **Speaker 3:** My name's Diep. I work as a lab technician at the hospital. Yesterday another employee spilled some water on the floor. I didn't see it and I slipped on the floor. I fell and hurt my back. Now, I can't move very well. What can I do?

**Narrator:** What can she do?

a. Say nothing, because she might lose her job.

b. Continue working. Ask another worker to do any heavy work for her.

c. Report the accident to the supervisor and go to the medical clinic.

d. Quit her job to recover from her back injury.

4. **Speaker 4:** I'm a housekeeper. My job is to clean the hotel rooms after the guests check out. I make the beds, vacuum, and clean the bathrooms. They gave me a new cleanser to use in the toilets and bathtubs. Last week I got a rash on my hands. It's red and sore. It hurts when I work. What can I do?

**Narrator:** What can she do?

a. Talk to her coworkers and see if they have the same problem.

b. Quit and look for a different job.

c. Not say anything and hope it goes away.

d. Discuss the problem with her coworkers and then with her supervisor.

## 9. Listening at Work: Safety Goals

**Narrator:** You are listening in on an end-of-year safety meeting. Mary Reynolds, Safety Coordinator, is speaking to department supervisors and safety representatives from every department. Listen to the information and take notes. Record the information in the chart.

**Mary Reynolds:** You all have in front of you our annual safety report. As you know, we have to improve our safety record. There were too many accidents in the past years.

These are our goals for the next year. Remember, our goal is to continue production but have fewer accidents.

1. Total work injuries and accidents: We need to reduce these by 20 percent. Next year there should be less than 35 accidents.

2. Accident investigation reports: Supervisors must investigate and report on all accidents within 24 hours.

3. Safety meetings: Every employee must know about the importance of safety. Supervisors must hold at least two safety meetings per month.

4. Machine safety: All machine safety checks on trucks, forklifts, and cranes must be completed by February 1.

5. Personal Protective Equipment: Workers must wear all necessary Personal Protective Equipment at all times. There will be no exceptions. Workers not wearing the required safety equipment will be sent home without pay.

6. Training classes for overhead crane operators will begin January 1. Please make sure all the people in your department attend the training. Completion of training is required before anyone can operate an overhead crane. Remember, January 1st. Are there any questions?

Total injuries and accidents (*not more than*) _____

Accident investigation reports (*completed within*) _____

Safety meetings (*how many*) _____

Machine safety (*completed by*) _____

Personal Protective Equipment (*who must wear; what happens if they don't*) _____

_____

training classes (*when and for who*) _____

_____

# ► Chapter 8: Labor Unions, Labor Laws, and Benefits

## 6. B. Discrimination and Equal Rights Protections

*Narrator:* Work in a group of four. Listen to each speaker. Then discuss the kind of discrimination experienced, the law violated, and what each person can do.

1. *Goi:* I'm Goi. I'm a dental receptionist. I'm handicapped. My legs are paralyzed so I have to sit in one place. I've been working in this office for about six months. I answer the phone, make appointments, and do the billing. Last week my boss told me he wanted me to help him clean out some cabinets. He wanted me to get up and down to clean! I couldn't do it. Now he says he'll fire me because I can't do the work.

   *Narrator:*
   What kind of discrimination did Goi report?
   What additional information do you need to investigate the problem?
   Was a law violated?
   What do you suggest she do?

2. *Samuel:* My name is Samuel. I'm a sales representative for a large medical company. I sell medical supplies and equipment. I visit doctors at their offices and talk to them on the phone. I get a fixed salary and a commission, the same as the other men and women in my department. For the last two months my sales have been the lowest in our office. What can I do? Some doctors just aren't buying new machines. They say the costs are too high. My boss says if my sales don't go up this month, he will cut my pay. But we're all supposed to get the same pay!

   *Narrator:*
   What kind of discrimination did Samuel report?
   What additional information do you need to investigate the problem?
   Was a law violated?
   What do you suggest he do?

3. *Olga:* My name's Olga. I'm 25 years old. I've tried to get a job as a telephone repair person for the last two years. The company says there are no openings, but I know that's not true. Two men in the training class with me have already been hired and we all applied at the same time.

   *Narrator:*
   What kind of discrimination did Olga report?
   What additional information do you need to investigate the problem?
   Was a law violated?
   What do you suggest she do?

4. *Esther:* Well, this is the way I heard the story. A man at our company was ready to be promoted to top management. He had 15 years' experience. He knew the job backward and forward. He was 55 years old. But they passed him over and promoted a younger man! They said he wasn't qualified for the management job! But really they just decided he was too old.

   *Narrator:*
   What kind of discrimination did Esther report?
   What additional information do you need to investigate the problem?
   Was a law violated?
   What do you suggest the older man do?

## 8. A. Understanding the Workplace: Full Time and Part Time Work

*Narrator:* Listen to the conversation. Discuss the questions with a partner.

*Sayeed:* Mr. Chang, could I talk with you?
*Mr. Chang:* Yes, Sayeed, what is it about?
*Sayeed:* I need a full-time job. Are there any openings?
*Mr. Chang:* How many hours are you working?
*Sayeed:* I've been working 20 hours some weeks and other weeks, 30 hours.
*Mr. Chang:* Why do you need a full-time job?
*Sayeed:* I need to earn more money to support my family. My children need to go to the doctor and we don't have any medical insurance.

**Mr. Chang:** I'm sorry, but there aren't any full-time openings now. When we have an opening, I'll keep you in mind.

**Sayeed:** Thanks. I'd really appreciate that.

**Narrator:**

What is Sayeed's problem?

Did Mr. Chang offer him a full time job?

What did the employer suggest about the future?

What do you think will happen?

★ Is it a good idea to ask the boss for more hours? more pay? more overtime? Why?

## 10. A. Listening at Work: Benefits

**Narrator:** As you listen to the conversation, take notes on the benefits and the dates.

1. **Rashid:** Ms. Blake?

   **Ms. Blake:** Yes, Rashid. What can I do for you?

   **Rashid:** I want to talk to you about my vacation days. I want to take my vacation from July 5 to July 9.

   **Ms. Blake:** Let me check our department's vacation schedule. Yes, those dates are open. I'll write in your vacation for the week of July 5 to 9.

   **Rashid:** Will I get my vacation pay before I go or after I come back?

   **Ms. Blake:** You'll get paid in the check after you return.

   Benefit _____

   Dates _____

2. **Narrator:** Lam is talking to the secretary about an error in his paycheck.

   **Lam:** I was out sick for two days the last pay period, but there is no sick pay on my check stub.

**Secretary:** Let me check my records. Yes. You were out two days, March 1 and March 2. The money should show on your paycheck and on your pay stub.

**Lam:** There's nothing here on my check.

**Secretary:** Let me see. Yes, you're right. It wasn't posted. I'll make an adjustment on your next check.

**Lam:** When will I get that money?

**Secretary:** In your next paycheck, in two weeks. Sorry about that.

**Lam:** It's Okay. Thanks for checking.

Benefit _____

Dates _____

3. **Tom:** You get Christmas off with pay and New Year's off with pay.

   **Mannie:** You mean we get paid for those days and we don't have to work?

   **Tom:** Yes. And you get four other paid holidays every year. It's in the union contract.

   **Mannie:** That's great! What do you want to do on New Year's Day?

   Benefit _____

   Dates _____

4. **Lydia:** Do you remember what happened when you were pregnant? You had to keep going back to the doctor.

   **Adriana:** Yeah. My ankles were swollen and I was always exhausted. I'm glad I could see the doctor so often while I was pregnant.

   Benefit _____

   Dates _____

<u>MY QUESTIONS</u>:

1. Will I have opportunities to take on other contracts?
2. Will I get an identification card?
3. Does this division of the college provide continuing education in the form of in-services and opportunities for all the instructors to get to know one another and even learn from one another?
4. How and when are evaluations conducted

<u>STANDARD QUESTIONS</u>
1. Tell me about yourself?

I am an experienced ESL teacher with a theoretical background in applied linguistics which includes the study of second language acquisition theory, grammar, testing and curriculum development, phonetics and phonology.

I have the opportunity to work in various types of programs ranging from more academic to literacy oriented programs. I started teaching ESL while I was getting a secondary education degree in Puerto Rico. I taught two 12th grade ESL classes for my teaching practicum. After I graduated I went to Michigan State to continue with a masters in Teaching English as a second language. While I was there I taught writing and grammar in their intensive English program. Before transferring to UIC I taught ESL in a community education program and I also did corporate training for College of Dupage Business Professional Institute. For COD I taught three different ESL classes at company called Concentric. My lowest level consisted mostly of Hispanic males who were preliterate and spoke very little English, so I focused on survival skills and reading readiness skills and building vocabulary. In the higher levels we were able to work on developing oral communication and reading and writing. In all of positions I have been responsible for daily lesson planning, assessment, and placement testing.

I enjoy my work because I find second language acquisition is never boring. I enjoy the challenge of effectively applying SLA theory to the classroom . I enjoy working with culturally and linguistically diverse people and find that there enthusiam to learn inspires me to be continue learning myself so that I can be the most effective teacher I can be.

Workplace training in particular can be especially gratifying for a few reasons. For one, when the program is effective there is immediate feedback from management because they notice the difference in the employees. Also there is another dimension added on to my job description and that I become a linguistic and cultural laison. If there is important company information that my students should many times it could be filtered through me and I incorporate into my teaching. I have also seen how my classes have actually improved relationships between workers of different linguistic and ethnic backgrounds simply because they interacted with one another until being in my class.

I think workplace literacy is somewhat an untapped topic in the TESOL literature, I aspire to contribute to this body of literature if given the opportunity. Developing inter-cultural awareness.

2. WHAT ARE YOUR STRENGTHS?

I believe greatest strengths draw on past experience. For one I am bilingual and bicultural and therefore can identify with many students on a cultural level. Like my students, I became this way through second language learning experience that was equally challenging. So, I know first hand the difficulties of second language learning the process of acculturation which is different from assimilation. As a veteran of the US army I am not intimated to be in male dominated work environment and understand the importance of commanding respect. As a seasoned ESL instructor, I familiar with different cultural learning styles and the importance and role culture play in learning.

3. WHAT ARE YOUR WEAKNESESS?

Chocalate is a weakness, but I am working on eating less of it and exercising more. I am very creative and I enjoy developing my own material so it is very easy for to spend a lot of time developing materials and then neglect personal objective such as working out or cleaning the house.

4. WHY DID YOU CHOOSE THIS CAREER

When I moved to Puerto Rico, I did not know Spanish at all. Unfortunately, for me there was not a Spanish Second language program so I was essentially thrusted into a sink or swim situation. I would have indeed sunk had it not been for a ESL teacher who understood my situation modified my academic program so that it was more adequate for a second language learning. Although I may not get paid very much I know the importance of my job and I truly get great satisfaction from helping people to achieve their goals. Many people leave their job everyday knowing that they are their because it pays the bills, they may even hate what they do. I on the other hand leave my job with a smile on my face and great stories to share.

5. WHAT ARE YOUR CAREER GOALS

I would like to eventually obtain a full time position as a ESL instructor   at a college or language consultant position at a corporate business/company

6. WHAT ARE YOUR SHORT_TERM GOALS

TO take on more contracts Find another job that does not conflict

7. ARE YOU A TEAM PLAYER?

8. Team teaching at Michigan State, Use thematic approach /

9. WHY SHOULD I HIRE YOU?

I have experience teaching adults in the workplace
Having degree in education and TESOL, I am very knowledgeable of Second language acquisition theory and practice, I am comfortable teaching GRAMMAR EITHER proactively or reactively. I can easily incorporate the clients objectives into the language curriculum and in fact it makes the teaching/learning process easier if there are set competencies that need to be achieved. I am understand the